T0318805

New Health Systems

Health Industrialization Set

coordinated by
Bruno Salgues

New Health Systems

*Integrated Care and Health
Inequalities Reduction*

Mohamed Lamine Bendaoud
Stéphane Callens

ELSEVIER

First published 2017 in Great Britain and the United States by ISTE Press Ltd and Elsevier Ltd

ISTE Press Ltd
27-37 St George's Road
London SW19 4EU
UK

www.iste.co.uk

Elsevier Ltd
The Boulevard, Langford Lane
Kidlington, Oxford, OX5 1GB
UK

www.elsevier.com

Notices

For information on all our publications visit our website at http://store.elsevier.com/

British Library Cataloguing-in-Publication Data
A CIP record for this book is available from the British Library
Library of Congress Cataloging in Publication Data
A catalog record for this book is available from the Library of Congress
ISBN 978-1-78548-165-9

Printed and bound in the UK and US

Contents

Acknowledgements

This report was written based on the studies of different health systems carried out by the LEM (UMR 9221 CNRS). The principal collaborators were:

Inequalities study (France, financed by CPER État/Région Hauts-de-France): Nezha Khallaf-Souilmi, Lou Shang, Jérome Longuépée and Anne-Charlotte Taillandier.

Haiti study (financed by ANR): Nezha Khallaf-Souilmi, Nikki Blackwell, Marie Christine Delauche, Joël Muller, Thierry Allafort-Duverger and Hervé Le Perff.

Sahel study: Josiane Gnassou (Thesis).

Introduction

New Healthcare Systems

We can talk about new health systems today thanks to a series of transformations that have taken place: the changing nature of diseases, changes in approaches toward caregiving and steering healthcare systems, as well as changes resulting from the integration of new technologies (instant communication of medical data from a person, remote management of therapeutic protocols, new coordination systems in health services). All the aspects of health systems have been influenced by these ongoing changes:

– Spatial dimension. The topic of "global health" emerged toward the end of the last millennium, after a series of global outbreak alerts. According to the World Health Organization (WHO), about 400 million people across the world are still cut off from access to any healthcare services. However, it is possible to attain the goal of universal health coverage using the existing systems, and this goal features in the United Nations Sustainable Development Goals 2015–2030.

– The organizational dimension is affected by the change in the respective proportions of different disorders. The relative share of infectious diseases fell sharply during the 20th Century. Providing services for people suffering from non-communicable pathologies requires better coordination between the healthcare and social approaches. Patients and the people around them are often required to be more active in the prevention or in the treatment of disorders that are related to lifestyle (food habits, regularly taking medication, staying active/exercising, etc.). Organizational gains are especially prominent in the steering of different healthcare services: the approach is consensual, progressive and prioritizes common interests.

– The way health and illness are experienced changes over a person's lifetime. "Connected health" also introduces changes. New technologies result in more mobile aids for patients. One of the factors contributing to this change is the possibility of ensuring a continuous surveillance of vital parameters without placing too many restrictions on an individual. The improvement in survival rates following a health problem modifies life experiences. People experience different health problems and will often have to live longer with several long-term illnesses.

Integrated people-centered health has been prioritized by the WHO, which established a working group focusing on this goal for the coming years. While the aim is undoubtedly to broadly set a course toward this goal, there is no guarantee that the ongoing transformations will actually follow the directions set out by the international organization.

I.1. Integrated people-centered health services

The intuitive definition of integrated health services is that of good internal cooperation within the healthcare system along with an assurance of continuity in care. The "integrated care" policy seeks to avoid the following dysfunctional features of health systems:

– erratic re-directions across the healthcare system;

– breaks in continuity during handovers;

– unnecessary duplication of procedures or investigations;

– repetitive consultations with specialists, each working in isolation;

– the inability to meet the needs of patients.

Integrated healthcare brings together coordination and medical ethics, as seen in the schema proposed by Contandriopoulos *et al.* [CON 01] when this method was introduced. The schema depicts an integrated healthcare system as being made up of three sub-systems: a value system, governance or management, and the clinical system.

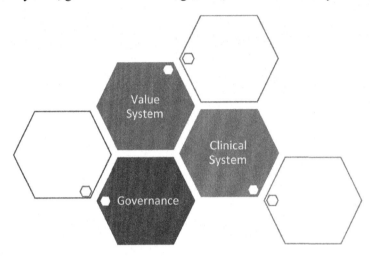

Figure I.1. *The three components of integrated healthcare*

A professional ethics charter for integrated health services was proposed by an academic journal dedicated to integrated health services [MIN 16]. It provides standardized content for the "Values" sub-system in the schema for the three components of integrated care (Figure I.1). According to this, integrated healthcare is:

1) Non-selective. It is a commitment to universal health coverage. It assures complete and adequate healthcare to meet the constantly evolving health needs and aspirations of individuals and populations.

2) Equitable. Healthcare is accessible and available to all.

3) Sustainable. Healthcare is both effective and efficient and contributes to sustainable development.

4) Coordinated. Health services are integrated around the needs of the population. Efficient collaboration is established between different care providers.

5) Continuous. Continuity of care and services across the course of a person's life are assured.

6) Comprehensive. Integrated healthcare does not dissociate the different components of health: physical, socio-economic, mental and emotional.

7) Preventive. Social determinants for poor health are approached through intra- and inter-sectional approaches that favor public health and the promotion of health.

8) "Empowering". Integrated healthcare strives to increase the power people have over their own lives, encouraging people to manage and take on responsibility for their health.

9) Focused on the manner in which people take decisions regarding healthcare, evaluating results and measuring success.

10) Respectful of the dignity of individuals, social conditions and cultural sensibilities.

11) Collaborative. Integrated healthcare promotes team work and collaboration between primary, secondary and tertiary health services as well as the establishment of relations with other sectors.

12) Co-produced. Integrated healthcare leads to the development of active partnerships with people and communities at the individual, organizational and political level.

13) Well-founded. Integrated healthcare is provided while respecting the rights and responsibilities that all citizens have a right to expect.

14) Governed by shared responsibility between care providers for the quality of care and the health results for local populations.

15) Based on evidence. Integrated healthcare policies and strategies are guided by the best available data and are supported over time by the evaluation of measurable objectives in order to improve quality and results.

16) Led by a consideration of the interconnectedness of systems.

The website for the WHO gives the following definition for integrated healthcare: *"Integrated health services encompasses the management and delivery of quality and safe health services so that people receive a continuum of health promotion, disease prevention, diagnosis, treatment, disease-management, rehabilitation and palliative care services, through the different levels and sites of care within the health system, and according to their needs throughout the life course. WHO is supporting countries in implementing people-centred and integrated health services by way of developing policy options, reform strategies, evidence-based guidelines and best practices that can be tailored to various country settings"* (WHO website, consulted March 28th 2017).

These different definitions are complementary. They provide updated content on professional ethics and organizational systems. However, they provide very little information on the specific content of integrated health services. Health services have, historically, been organized around acute pathological episodes. In the integrated health services approach, these organizational improvements are integrated into the framework of current professional ethics. "People-centered health services" goes beyond a vision of innovation as being limited only to technological aspects. The organizational rules proposed here draw from organizational literature that is common to quality and risk-management policies.

I.2. Historical counter-currents across healthcare systems

The wide variety of healthcare systems around the world today can be explained by the sheer number of factors related to the construction of healthcare systems: prioritizing the patient (clinical system) or norms (bureaucracy); services for all citizens (Beveridge) or for employees only (Bismarck); health systems that were built through philanthropic means and others that are a network of health workers; a more or less distinct role of *gatekeeper*; and a disconnect between the social, mental health and healthcare services. However, healthcare services today borrow from all these systems and are the sum of elements that come from varied options.

The history of the WHO is itself marked by shifts between periods where the international organization dedicated itself principally to selective programs (for example, the fight against malaria) and periods where a non-selective strategy was chosen. Schematically, the organization went through four phases of this kind. Before the Alma-Alta declaration of 1978, the activities of the WHO were influenced by infectious diseases. This declaration, the blueprint for a primary healthcare program, represented the first turning point for the organization. It was justified by the results of the fight against malaria, which questioned the appropriateness of the selective, or disease-by-disease, approach. The Bamako initiative of 1987 marked the return to a biomedical paradigm, with the possibility of financing coming directly from the patients. The recurrent problem faced by the WHO in the management of epidemics (influenza, Ebola hemorrhagic fever) laid the ground for another shift: the 2000–2015 United Nations Millennium Development Goals (MDG) approached the subject of health through programs dedicated to pathologies (HIV/AIDS, tuberculosis), while the 2015–2030 Sustainable Development Goals program is based on a non-selective formulation – universal healthcare (point 3.8 of the SDG), which recently complemented the integrated healthcare framework promoted by the WHO.

The Alma-Alta Declaration on Primary Healthcare of September 12, 1978

I. The Conference strongly reaffirms that health, which is a state of complete physical, mental and social wellbeing, and not merely the absence of disease or infirmity, is a fundamental human right, and that the attainment of the highest possible level of health is the most important worldwide social goal, whose realization requires the action of many other social and economic sectors in addition to the health sector.

II. The existing gross inequality in the health status of the people particularly between developed and developing countries as well as within countries is politically, socially and economically unacceptable and is, therefore, of common concern to all countries.

III. Economic and social development, based on a New International Economic Order, is of basic importance to the fullest attainment of health for all and to the reduction of the gap between the health status of the developing and developed countries. The promotion and protection of the health of the people is essential to sustained economic and social development and contributes to a better quality of life and to world peace.

IV. The people have the right and duty to participate individually and collectively in the planning and implementation of their healthcare.

V. Governments have a responsibility for the health of their people, which can be fulfilled only by the provision of adequate health and social measures. A main social target of governments, international organizations and the whole world community in the coming decades should be the attainment by all peoples of the world by the year 2000 of a level of health that will permit them to lead a socially and economically productive life. Primary healthcare is the key to attaining this target as part of development in the spirit of social justice.

VI. Primary healthcare is essential healthcare based on practical, scientifically sound and socially acceptable methods and technology made universally accessible to individuals and families in the community through their full participation and at a cost that the community and country can afford to maintain at every stage of their development in the spirit of self-reliance and self-determination. It forms an integral part both of the country's health system, of which it is the central function and main focus, and of the overall social and economic development of the community. It is the first level of contact of individuals, the family and community with the national health system bringing healthcare as close as possible to where people live and work, and constitutes the first element of a continuing healthcare process.

Mintzberg [MIN 79] drew up a list of coordination mechanisms: the market, the company (hierarchy and consensus) and different approaches to normalization (through regulations, through ethics). These coordination mechanisms seem to be a growing concern in the history of healthcare systems. In this field, Mintzberg's list has been worked on in a cumulative process. The standardization of skills accompanied medical specialization in the development of hospital structures. The Alma-Alta declaration standardized a list of primary products alone. For example, child and maternal care figure in this minimal list of "essential health services". The organizational mode that resulted from the Alma-Alta declaration was more bureaucratic in nature – a model of public health dispensed by healthcare workers. The Bamako initiative reintroduced organizations and costs. The "Managed Care" model is one way of deploying coordination mechanisms, based on companies that take charge of both the financing and delivery of care services. During the MDG period, the WHO worked on updating the Health Code, bringing about standardization through regulations. The shift during the ODD phase prioritizes standardization brought about through professional ethics and research into organizational gains through new internal collaborations in the healthcare system.

Period	Phase	Coordination method
Pre-Alma –Alta declaration (< 1978)	Selective	Standardization of skills in medical specializations
Between Alma-Alta and Bamako (1987)	Non-selective	Bureaucracy, public health system managed by health workers
HIV/AIDS epidemic, MDG	Selective	Calling on the market, Managed Care ; standardization through Health Regulations
2015 : SDG, universal access to healthcare	Non-selective	Standardization through ethics, good practice. Strengthening internal collaboration within healthcare systems.

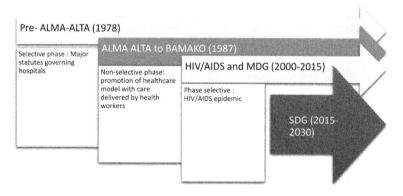

Figure I.2. *Schema showing the succession of coordination methods recommended by the WHO*

I.3. Health inequalities

A comparative analysis of the texts that make up the Alma-Alta Declaration of 1978 and the WHO's 2015 Framework for Integrated Healthcare Services shows a continuity in the directions chosen by the organization, through the priority given to the primary line of care (general practitioners, health workers) over the second and third lines (principally regional hospitals and specialized hospitals). The benchmark healthcare systems for good practices have a very high percentage of primary response levels (95% in Sweden, for instance). A technical ratio of "doctors per bed" indicates that health is knowledge-intensive, and that the performance of healthcare systems improves as the doctor-to-bed ratio in turn improves.

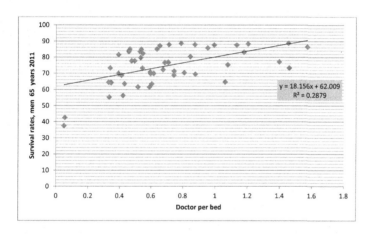

Figure I.3. *Performance of healthcare systems based on the "doctor-to-bed" ratio (source: World Bank Database, series SH.MED.PHYS.ZS and SH.MED.BEDS.ZS)*

Actions taken to reduce health inequalities may be divided into three categories: *upstream* (usually focused on general lifestyle factors), *intermediary* (based on specific, identified risk factors) and *downstream* (focused on conditions of access to and the quality of care). Local conditions determine the choice of action. For example, improving the quality of the water supply to agricultural communities would be more effective than providing antibiotic medication (an *upstream* policy); similarly, it would be better to implement a follow up with patients (*downstream* policy), or to implement a policy based on specific risks (for example, vaccination against a pathogen).

Strategies, policy options and interventions for the framework on integrated, people-centered health services (extracts)

(Document OMS EB 138/37, 18 December 2015)

Strategy 1: Empowering and engaging people and communities

Empowering and engaging people is about providing the opportunity, skills and resources that people need to be articulate and empowered users of health services. It is also about reaching the underserved and marginalized groups of the population in order to guarantee universal access to and benefit from services that are co-produced according to their specific needs.

1.1 Empowering and engaging individuals and families. (…) individuals and families need to be active participants.

ACTIONS: • health education • shared clinical decision-making between individual, families, carers and providers • self-management including personal care assessment and treatment plans, • knowledge of health system navigation • patient satisfaction surveys

1.2 Empowering and engaging communities.

(…) ACTIONS • community-delivered care • community health workers • development of civil society

1.3 Empowering and engaging informal carers.

(…) ACTIONS: • training for informal carers, informal carer networks • peer support and expert patient groups • caring for the carers • respite care

1.4 Reaching the underserved and marginalized.

This approach is of paramount importance for guaranteeing universal access to health services. It is essential for fulfilling broader societal goals such as equity, social justice and solidarity, and helps to create social cohesion. It requires actions at all levels of the health sector and concerted action with other sectors and all segments of society, in order to address the other determinants of health and health equity.

ACTIONS • integration of health equity goals into health sector objectives • provision of outreach services for the underserved including mobile units, transport systems and telemedicine • contracting out of services when warranted • expansion of primary care-based systems

Strategy 2: Strengthening governance and accountability

Strengthening governance requires a participatory approach to policy formulation, decision-making and performance evaluation at all levels of the health system, from policy-making to the clinical intervention level.

2.1 Bolstering participatory governance. (…)

ACTIONS • community participation in policy formulation and evaluation • national health policies, strategies and plans promoting integrated people-centered health services • harmonization and alignment of donor programs with national policies, strategies and plans • decentralization, where appropriate, to local levels • clinical governance

2.2 Enhancing mutual accountability. Essentially, this means answerability of decision-making, and encompasses both the "rendering of the account" (that is, providing information about performance) and the "holding to account" (namely, the provision of rewards and sanctions). (…)

ACTIONS: health rights and entitlement • provider report cards • patient-reported outcomes and balanced scorecard • performance-based financing and contracting • population registration with accountable care provider(s)

Strategy 3: Reorienting the model of care

Reorienting the model of care means ensuring that efficient and effective healthcare services are designed, purchased and provided through innovative models of care that prioritize primary and community care services and the co-production of health. This encompasses the shift from inpatient to outpatient and ambulatory care. It requires investment in holistic and comprehensive care, including health promotion and ill-health prevention strategies that support people's health and well-being. It also respects gender and cultural preferences in the design and operation of health services.

3.1 Defining service priorities based on life-course needs, respecting people's preferences. This approach means appraising the package of health services offered at different levels of the care delivery system, covering the entire life course. It uses a blend of methods to understand both the particular health needs of the population, including social preferences, and the cost effectiveness of alternative health interventions, guiding decision-making on allocation of resources to healthcare. It also includes health technology assessment.

ACTIONS • local health needs assessment • comprehensive packaging of services for all population groups • gender, cultural and age-sensitive services • health technology assessment

3.2 Revaluing promotion, prevention and public health. This approach means placing increased emphasis and resources on promotive, preventive and public health services. Public health systems include all public, private, and voluntary entities that contribute to the delivery of essential public health functions within a defined geographical area.

ACTIONS • monitoring population health status • population risk stratification • surveillance, research and control of risks and threats to public health • improved financial and human resources allocated to health promotion and disease prevention • public health regulation and enforcement

3.3 Building strong primary care-based systems. Strong primary care services are essential for reaching the entire population and guaranteeing universal access to services. Building such services involves ensuring adequate funding, appropriate training, and connections to other services and sectors. This approach promotes coordination and continuous care over time for people with complex health problems, facilitating intersectoral action in health. It calls for interprofessional teams to ensure the provision of comprehensive services for all. It prioritizes community and family-oriented models of care as a mainstay of practice with a focus on disease prevention and health promotion.

ACTIONS • primary care services with a family and community-based approach • multidisciplinary primary care teams • family medicine • gatekeeping to access other specialized services • greater proportion of health expenditure allocated to primary care

3.4 Shifting toward more outpatient and ambulatory care

Service substitution is the process of replacing some forms of care with those that are more efficient for the health system. The approach means finding the right balance between primary care, specialized outpatient care and hospital inpatient care, recognizing that each has an important role within the healthcare delivery system.

ACTIONS • home care, nursing homes and hospices • repurposing secondary and tertiary hospitals for acute complex care only • outpatient surgery • day hospitals • progressive patient

3.5 Innovating and incorporating new technologies. Rapid technological change is enabling the development of increasingly innovative care models. New information and communication technologies allow new types of information integration. When used appropriately, they can assure continuity of information, track quality, facilitate patients' empowerment and reach geographically isolated communities.

ACTIONS • shared electronic medical record • telemedicine • mHealth

Strategy 4: Coordinating services within and across sectors

Services should be coordinated around the needs and demands of people. This result requires integration of healthcare providers within and across healthcare settings, development of referral systems and networks among levels of care, and the creation of linkages between health and other sectors. It encompasses intersectoral action at the community level in order to address the social determinants of health and optimize use of scarce resources, including, at times, through partnerships with the private sector. Coordination does not necessarily require the merging of the different structures, services or workflows, but rather focuses on improving the delivery of care through the alignment and harmonizing of the processes and information among the different services.

4.1 Coordinating care for individuals. Coordination of care is not a single activity, but rather a range of strategies that can help achieve better continuity of care and enhance the patient's experience with services, particularly during care transitions. The focus for improvement is on the delivery of care to the individual, with services coordinated around their needs and those of their families. This approach also covers improved information flows and maintenance of trustworthy relationships with providers over time.

ACTIONS • care pathways • referral and counter-referral systems • health navigators • case management • improved care transition • team-based care

4.2 Coordinating health programs and providers. This approach includes bridging the administrative, informational and funding gaps between levels of care and providers. This involves sector components such as pharmaceutical and product safety regulators, information technology teams working with disease surveillance systems, allied health teams delivering treatment plans in collaboration with each other, disease-specific laboratory services linked to broader services improvement, and provider networks focused on closer relationships in patient care.

ACTIONS • regional or district-based health service delivery networks • purchasing integrated services • integrating vertical programs into national health systems • incentives for care coordination

4.3 Coordinating across sectors. Successful coordination in health matters involves multiple actors, both within and beyond the health sector. It encompasses sectors such as social services, finance, education, labor, housing, the private sector and law enforcement, among others. It necessitates strong leadership from the health ministry to coordinate intersectoral action, including coordination for early detection and rapid response to health crises.

ACTIONS • health in all policies • intersectoral partnerships • merging of health sector with social services • working with education sector to align professional curriculum toward new skills needed • integrating traditional and complementary medicine with modern health systems • coordinating preparedness and response to health crises

Strategy 5: Creating an enabling environment

In order for the four previous strategies to become an operational reality, it is necessary to create an enabling environment that brings together all stakeholders to undertake transformational change. This complex task will involve a diverse set of processes to bring about the necessary changes in leadership and management, information systems, methods to improve quality, reorientation of the workforce, legislative frameworks, financial arrangements, and incentives.

5.1 Strengthening leadership and management for change.

New forms of collaborative leadership that help to bring together multiple stakeholders are needed for successful reform of health services. All healthcare professionals, and especially clinicians, need to be engaged in management and leadership for change in continuous partnership with local communities. Achieving people-centered and integrated care requires the application of complex processes and service innovations that warrant an underlying change management strategy.

ACTIONS • transformational and distributed leadership • change management strategies

5.2 Strengthening information systems and knowledge management. Development of information systems and an organizational culture that supports monitoring and evaluation, knowledge sharing and using data in decision-making is also a prerequisite for transformational change.

ACTIONS • development of information systems • systems research • knowledge management

5.3 Striving for quality improvement and safety. Institutions and providers need to strive constantly for quality improvement and safety. These efforts include both technical and perceived quality.

ACTIONS • quality assurance • creating a culture of safety • continuous quality improvement

5.4 Reorienting the health workforce. Special attention needs to be given to readying the health workforce with an appropriate skills mix in order to equitably and sustainably meet the population's health needs. Health workers must be organized into teams and supported with adequate processes of work, clear roles and expectations, guidelines, opportunities to correct competency gaps, supportive feedback, fair wage, and a suitable work environment and incentives.

ACTIONS • tackling health workforce shortages and maldistribution • health workforce training • multi-professional teams working across organizational boundaries • improving working conditions and compensation mechanisms • provider support groups • strengthening professional associations

5.5. Aligning regulatory frameworks. Regulation plays a key role in establishing the rules within which professionals and organizations must operate within more people-centered and integrated health systems – for example, in terms of setting new quality standards and/or paying against performance targets.

ACTIONS • aligning regulatory framework

5.6 Improving funding and reforming payment systems. Changes in the way care is funded and paid for are also needed to promote adequate levels of funding and the right mix of financial incentives in a system that supports the integration of care between providers and settings and protection of patients against undue out-of-pocket expenditures on health.

ACTIONS • assuring sufficient health system financing and aligning resource allocation with reform priorities • mixed payment models based on capitation • bundled payments

Professional medical ethics are ethics related to the contingent decision of preserving equity. It introduces a set of actions to reduce health inequalities. The content of these actions depends on local parameters. However, the 1978 Declaration gives primary importance to upstream approaches. On the other hand, the 2015 document seems to prioritize downstream measures (for example, point 3.3. of the Framework on Integrated People-Centered Health Services "to guarantee universal health coverage"), in accordance with the Sustainable Development Goals proposed for the period 2015–2030 by the United Nations.

Schematically, the major international texts on the subject first focused on upstream measures (Alma-Alta declaration of 1978), passed through a phase of prioritizing intermediary measures (especially because of the HIV/AIDS pandemic), and then emphasized the need for downstream measures (Framework on Integrated People-Centered Health Services 2015). It is evident that structural factors (better infrastructure especially for water adduction and treatment) may come into play such that the optimal policy for reducing health inequalities shifts from an upstream approach to a downstream approach. However, we must be cautious about the effects of substitution (for example, better care in treating addiction resulting from an integrated health policy, combined with a decrease in incentives to reduce alcohol consumption).

The question that this book seeks to study is that of health inequalities in these new health systems, which are structured following the integrated health services approach. This question covers a much wider range of debates and interrogations, such as the changes in society from the new social networks or, again, as a result of a collaborative economy. The rolling out of "telemedicine" (exchanging electronic medical files, mobile health) on a global system is beset by delays and presupposes a system of coordination ("integrated care") that can implement it in accordance with medical ethics. While there are many positive examples of collaborative economy, from interconnected networks, the most important of which is the Cochrane Collaboration for professional document management, healthcare professionals are deeply concerned about the possible "uberization" of their field. These fears are further stocked by online healthcare services and regulation authorities who may set their objectives based on existing developed systems.

The book is divided into two parts. The first part offers an overview of the problem of inequalities in the field of health. The second part discusses sustainable and equitable architecture for health systems.

PART 1

Health Inequalities

The Origin of Inequality

Between the years 2000 and 2015, the average gain in life expectancy around the world was 5 years. The gap between the countries with the shortest and longest life expectancy at birth is 36 years, but the city of London alone shows a gap of 17 years from the same indicator, despite guaranteed universal health coverage. If two such widely contrasting countries such as Sweden and Bangladesh are compared over the period between 1990 and 2010, only Sweden shows an increase in prosperity. However, the performance indicator for the health systems (measured as the survival rate for males to the age of 65 years) registered much higher growth for Bangladesh than for Sweden. Along the axis showing the variations on the health indicator, there are some strongly negative trends (countries with a high incidence of HIV/AIDS) and some strongly positive trends (countries emerging from a civil war) without any corresponding variations in prosperity. An offset axis for the average growth value of the health indicator also shows large amplitude variations in prosperity (for example, a negative variation for mining-dependent countries whose resources have run out) which does not alter the progress on the health indicator.

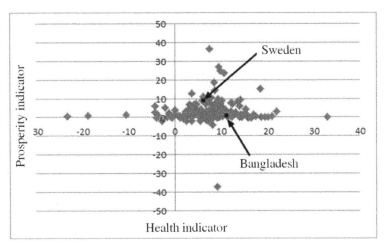

	Bangladesh	Sweden
Increase in per-capita GDP (expressed in purchasing power units / 1000)	0.73	9.56
Improvement in survival rate (male, younger than 65 years)	11.22 %	6.92 %

Figure 1.1. *Country-wise variations in prosperity and health (World, 1990–2010)*

Most countries fall into the upper right quadrant, with positive variations on both prosperity and health during the period from 1990 to 2010. The most intriguing explanations are also based on this conjoint rise in prosperity and health. Angus Deaton [DEA 13] highlights the novelty of having a greater number of people reach more advanced ages. At the same time, Richard Wilkinson [WIL 10] recognizes the smooth functioning of egalitarian societies (such as Sweden), which have combined improvements in prosperity and health. These interpretations are at quite a variance with the proposition made in Rousseau's [ROU 55] classic text on the origins of inequality, where he associates improved health with a return to nature.

J. J. Rousseau [ROU 55], *Discourse on the Origins and Fundamentals of Inequality among Men*, 1755 (extract).

With respect to sickness, I shall not repeat the vain and false declamations which most healthy people pronounce against medicine; but I shall ask if any solid observations have been made from which it may be justly concluded that, in the countries where the art of medicine is most neglected, the mean duration of man's life is less than in those where it is most cultivated. How indeed can this be the case, if we bring on ourselves more diseases than medicine can furnish remedies? The great inequality in manner of living, the extreme idleness of some, and the excessive labour of others, the easiness of exciting and gratifying our sensual appetites, the too exquisite foods of the wealthy which overheat and fill them with indigestion, and, on the other hand, the unwholesome food of the poor, often, bad as it is, insufficient for their needs, which induces them, when opportunity offers, to eat voraciously and overcharge their stomachs; all these, together with sitting up late, and excesses of every kind, immoderate transports of every passion, fatigue, mental exhaustion, the innumerable pains and anxieties inseparable from every condition of life, by which the mind of man is incessantly tormented; these are too fatal proofs that the greater part of our ills are of our own making, and that we might have avoided them nearly all by adhering to that simple, uniform and solitary manner of life which nature prescribed.

(p. 14, trans. by G.D.H. Cole, https://www.aub.edu.lb/fas/cvsp/Documents/DiscourseonInequality.pdf879500092.pdf)

1.1. A tale of two phases: an initial explosion followed by geographical redistribution

In Wilkinson's [WIL 10] work, inequality arises from penury. Other authors such as Jared Diamond [DIA 97] also associate the origin of inequality with Force, simple brutal appropriation. The question of the origin of inequalities is debated today using archeological data. It is seen that the first agricultural societies remained egalitarian, while a short transition period (the Chalcolithic period) caused a shift from this state of equality to the most manifest proofs of social inequality, as with the pyramids of the first Pharaohs of Egypt, for example. Rousseau blamed the emergence of the Civil Law and yet, issues from the archeological period in question accompany the emergence of a Public Law. The specific conventions of this period are the conventions for the limitation of Force, as with the institution of the Flower War of the Aztecs, for instance. While agriculture arose without any real understanding of technical power [CAU 00], inequality emerged the moment knowledge was recognized as being powerful. This can be seen through the changes in pantheons, for example. The pantheons of the earliest agricultural societies were simple, organized around nature spirits, while the pantheons of the Metal Age were built of polymath divinities with many diverse technical powers.

We live today in "knowledge societies", which are non-egalitarian. This has not come about through some historical accident, as the result of a particularly brutal conqueror or a particular episode of poverty.

Biologists make use of a "punctuated equilibrium model": phases of explosion interrupt very long periods where few things change. The period between the start of the Metal Ages and the age of Rousseau and the Encyclopédistes[1] constitutes one such long period of stability. Most of the technologies described by the Encyclopédistes of the 18th Century were introduced early in the Metal Ages: the wheel, writing systems, woven material, and animal traction. And so was inequality. There is evidence that allows us to conclusively date the emergence of inequality. The Varna civilization (in present-day Bulgaria) is the first known civilization in the European zone to have mastered the metalwork for gold and copper. Gold jewelry has been found in tombs, distributed in a very unequal fashion. Other Neolithic civilizations of the same period practiced funerary rites for their dead. While the fragmentary nature of archeological elements imposes great caution when interpreting the transition, when it comes to *dating* it, there is great certainty: inequality emerged during the transition from the Neolithic to the Metal Ages. One

---

1 Members of a French Writer's Society, led by Denis Diderot and Jean le Rond d'Alembert, who contributed articles to the ambitious *Encyclopédie, ou dictionnaire raisonné des sciences, des arts et des métiers*, which played a vital role in promoting rationalism and science in Europe during the Enlightenment period.

of the pieces of evidence of this transition period is a mummified body unearthed in the Alps, which dates to a period about 5,270 years ago. The corpse dates back to the Chalcolithic Age, the first Metal Age, and testifies to the man having died following a conflict that made use of copper weapons and sophisticated medical knowledge.

This constitutive and long-lasting regime of inequality belongs to traditional agricultural societies. These began to disappear very rapidly after the political and economic revolutions of the 18th Century. This new transition phase is undoubtedly still incomplete. The total inequality index, on a global scale, was rather low around the beginning of the 19th Century and is much higher today. This leads to a second debate concerning contemporary inequality and its origin in historical societies. Jared Diamond traces the origin of inequality to geographic factors, as present-day inequalities have a strongly geographical nature. Everyone knows about the satellite photographs that contrast the prosperity on one side of a border with the poverty on the other side, as with South and North Korea, for example. Given that there is a marked inequality from birth, arising from various social statuses, contemporary inequality is also based on place of birth.

1.2. An initial explosion: was Rousseau right?

There are several answers to the question on the origin of inequality. The oldest answer is the one proposed by Rousseau. According to Rousseau, "iron" preceded "wheat" and the inequality between men, farmers, may be traced back to the institution of property. Modern archeology, however, disproves these points, showing that the invention of agriculture was not accompanied by a recognition of the transformative power of technical developments. While Neolithic societies – the first agricultural societies – were organized by large collective rites, there was no real social hierarchy. The grand rituals allowed people to enter into the rhythm of all living things – men, plants and animals, all of which live and die. Private law did exist, and these primarily agrarian societies could, sometimes, survive for several millennia.

Inequality is one of the markers of the end of the Neolithic period. The first Metallurgic Age, made up of the Copper and Iron Ages, was a transition between the Neolithic period and the highly hierarchized societies of the later Bronze Age. Thus, the question of the origin of inequality has been precisely dated by archeology, with an egalitarian "wheat" age preceding a non-egalitarian "iron" age.

1.2.1. Archaeological data

The first human groups of the modern biological species were hunter-gatherers. They spread out over the globe, diversifying culturally. This diversification may have led to about 15,000 spoken languages, each with a very small group of speakers. The languages of the hunter-gatherers made it possible to adapt well to a given environment. The vocabulary to specify a common component from the environment would have been extraordinarily precise, with different terms designating animals that were not of the same age, a snowy coat covering the environment or a nutritive plant. Under conditions that remain mysterious, there was an episode of wide linguistic unification to introduce more conceptual communication devices: a single term for snow, understood by a large number of speakers. These linguistic tools established the principle of a socially stratified society.

Renfrew [REN 94] proposed a schema (oversimplified, no doubt) of linguistic unification by diffusion of Indo-European language in the European context. Archeological sites in present-day Belgium allow us to imagine the situation around 5000 BC. This was a "pioneer" context: pioneer farmers settled along large waterways and progressively cleared land, which was essentially forest land. Archeological sites provide evidence of armed conflicts with the occupants of this forest. The farmers succeeded in settling here and organizing resources such that the number of speakers of their language increased. Although this explanation is over-simplified, it allows us to introduce the two aspects of societies that are related to the emergence of inequality: on the one hand, we have the diversity of small groups of humans whose resources are primarily acquired through hunting and gathering; on the other hand, there are societies that resemble the village in the world of Asterix: some specialization, clearly defined professions such as the blacksmith, and social stratification, with the Druid being the repository of power in the village. Magical power resides in one social stratum, that of the Druids, such that, according to Caesar, they could order warriors to end combat.

The recognition of the power of knowledge came about in the first Metallurgic period, as can be seen through the representation of the gods: the first agrarian societies worshipped deities linked to natural cycles, while the first metallurgic societies have complex pantheons, where deities are associated with technical attributes. Archeologists state that "wheat" preceded "iron" and private law preceded the recognition of technical power, contrary to the "iron, wheat" sequence postulated by Rousseau.

Pre-Columbian societies testify to the conditions in which inequality emerged. An initial metallurgy was limited to goldsmithery: with neither tools nor arms being made. The economy remained barter-system driven. Peddlers would demonstrate their high social status by organizing potlatches, ostentatious consumption of their surplus goods. Economic actors in the Copper Age societies played no role in affirming social inequality.

The Flower War Agreements, which limited warrior operations, were the driving forces behind the emergence of private law and social stratification. Aztec society had a school, the Calmecac, reserved for the elite. Pierre Clastres concluded that there was no possibility of organized powers emerging from primitive warrior societies. An economy driven by the predation of small bands may endure, but without leading to complex social structures. An understanding between priests and warriors formed the foundation of Aztec society. One official historiography recalls the past of the Aztec warrior bands and thus justifies the existence of an aristocracy. Inequality was born of hierarchy, of the regulation of sacrificial power. It was institutionalized with the recognition of technical power and an affirmation of the social superiority of those who represented a spiritual power over those of the warrior class.

The Aztec Flower War conventions are a good example of the assertion of inequality in one of the Chalcolithic societies, the Copper Age society, at the overlapping point of the Neolithic period and the

Metallic Ages. Aztec society used only stone weapons, though their working of metals was highly developed. This anomaly is characteristic of this Chalcolithic period. The Flower War Agreement was a convention between cities that had difficulties in getting regular supplies. In the Aztec society, the highest importance was given to the priests, who could dismiss political powers. Through the Flower War Agreement, the wars between cities became a source of provisions for the cities: the prisoners were sacrificed and eaten.

In Ancient Egypt, the Pharaoh's crown symbolized the federation of the farmers of Upper Egypt and the artisans of Lower Egypt. The beginning of metallurgy increased the diversity by giving Lower Egypt an important economic role. The Crown thus transformed diversity into inequality. These changes also took place in a society with a level of technology, where the knowledge of metallurgy was used primarily for goldsmithery. Contrary to Aztec society, political power here dominated over the priests. Only fragments of Pre-Pharaonic Egypt remain, not providing adequate support of social differentiation. In the case of the Aztecs, political power was very weak, contrary to the all-powerful Pharaohs. However, in both cases, there was a similar transition from a situation of diversity to a situation of inequality, and in both the cases, it took place in the same technological age, when metallurgy was not used for producing arms, that is, the Chalcolithic Age.

Rousseau's *Discourse on Inequality* postulated three major elements: a driving force attributed to the modifications of civil institutions; a process presented as corruption following a growth in knowledge; and historical priority given to the metallurgy of ferrous metals. All this results in an aspiration for a simple lifestyle, and there is no practical impact of current medical knowledge, simply rules for living that lead to good health.

When compared with current archeological data, these propositions today seem strange. The situations that provided the context for the transition toward inequality are those of an initial diversity of populations with different civil institutions, some of whom would go on to have developed civil laws while others would not; management of a growing urbanization; situations where confined land was exploited (such as mountain territories), or the emergence of a new social diversity as a result of technological advancement toward the end of the Neolithic period.

Technical awareness emerged after large-scale clearing of land, which may have had a major impact on the environment. Similarly, social violence may have been worrying enough to bring about conventions that sought to limit the impact of the conflicts. A barrier effect was important for the transition between the hunter-gatherer economy and the start of a rudimentary agrarian economy. This barrier effect can be seen through the continued presence of the primary hunter-gatherer societies in today's world. Twenty percent of land surfaces today are still occupied exclusively by these aboriginal populations. The situation as far as the large Neolithic civilizations are concerned is completely different: there is often extensive archeological evidence of these civilizations, but a complete absence of any contemporary presence. They have completely disappeared. It is possible to refuse to transition to agriculture – there are indeed some major religions, such as Jainism, that refuse to make this transition. However, it is more difficult to imagine the shunning of the wheel, for instance. Neolithic sledges have left deep marks on the rocks of Malta; the practical advantages of the innovations that marked the end of the Neolithic period are very clear and may have facilitated the adoption of these inventions. The disappearance of all the great Neolithic civilizations (while some hunter-gatherer societies still endure) indicates the importance of the problems faced by cultures that carried out large programs to construct and modify their environment.

Archeological data indicate that medical knowledge was developed very early, especially with the development of pastoralism. The first European farmers, those of the Neolithic Pottery civilization, had advanced medicine, which allowed them, for example, to carry out surgical procedures as advanced as trepanations. Their demographic expansion was the result of a diet that incorporated animal milk and contradicted Rousseau's hypothesis of "the ills of civilization" spreading more rapidly than medical knowledge developed.

The empirically observed dynamic in the period 2000–2015 is a positive process of civilization: the average life span increasing by 5 years goes against Rousseau's hypothesis of a negative dynamic of illnesses brought about by civilization. In addition, the explanations provided by Rousseau for the emergence of inequality no longer correspond with the archeological data available.

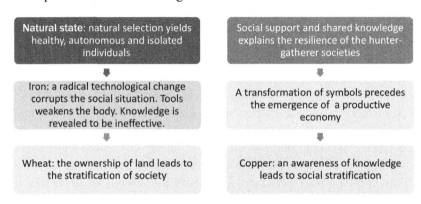

Figure 1.2. *The path to inequality as stated by Rousseau (left) and as determined from archeological data (right)*

1.3. Inequality became geographical: is Diamond right?

When Pareto studied societies at the beginning of the 20th Century, he made the general observation that internal inequality (some rich people, many poor people) was common around the world whether it was Dresden, Lausanne or Buenos Aires. A century later, the contemporary world can highlight inequality between countries: the whole population of Norway is comfortably off, while the population of the Republic of Haiti is very poor. Inequalities have modified themselves structurally, with very marked differences between different regions of the world and within these regions themselves. Africa is the poorest continent, while South America is the most unequal.

Mike Davis' polemical work on *Tropical Genocides* [DAV 01] introduces the question of the origin of inequality in its contemporary global form. Davis puts forward several assertions: the key role of climatic extremes in the major crises at the end of the Victorian era as well as poor governance of the colonial empires that presided over the beginning of the stratification of different parts of the world. Colonization may have formed the basis for global inequality. As in Diamond's work, two elements are put forward to explain inequality: one theory speaks of absolute advantages and disadvantages, and another relates superior social status to the use of force. One of the weaknesses in Davis' presentation is that while his work is situated in a period of closed global markets, with the rise in protectionism that followed the Civil War in the United States, he omitted the heavy taxation on commercial trade in his explanations. The period chosen is also that in which, for the first time, there were large growth rates – and this is an important factor in explaining global inequalities.

1.3.1. *Absolute advantages and disadvantages*

In this theory, inequalities reflect localized natural characteristics: country X is rich because it has abundant mineral resources, and country Y is poor as it is subject to repeated catastrophes. This poverty linked to catastrophes is only seen in insular economies with very short periods between catastrophic events. However, the explanation is not universally applicable: human mobility is such that the most inhospitable countries are abandoned or poorly inhabited. Spreading habitation is not conducive to managing major risks, for example, a forest is weakened by invasive habitation. However, the explanation rests primarily on a psychological factor: the major risk was underestimated during the decision to settle in this location.

Overexposed zones are sometimes very attractive: a magnificent little island in the middle of the Pacific, or a high valley in the mountains. This effect of peace and calm attracts a population that is more comfortably off than the average population – thus, after cyclone Andrew passed through Florida, more than 50% of the first new constructions in the zones of destruction were organized by a population that was wealthier than the earlier inhabitants. Here also the psychological aspect of how the environment is perceived seems significant.

Collier [COL 08] postulates four explanations for the situation of immense poverty of the "bottom billion", the billion poorest inhabitants of the planet. The four factors are bad governance, civil war, landlocked countries and the "resource curse". The last two factors are linked to geography. However, with appropriate infrastructure – roads, railways, canals and harbor agreements – the effects of being landlocked can be mitigated. "Resource curse" is a situation created by an oligarchy that is fed by mining-dependent income. The certainty of financial resources that come from oil, for example, leads to the absence of any development policy put in place by the ruling class. In this case, the geographical advantage turns out to be a disadvantage. The frequency of this reversal is enough to make the relationship between geographic and environmental factors and inequalities quite complex.

1.3.2. *Force as the foundation of inequality*

Force is the explanation used as the last resort to explain observed inequalities. Diamond proposes that the use of weapons was the cause of the Spanish victory over the Aztecs. The Aztec rules of combat were, in fact, the determining factor: Cortès took advantage of the internal weaknesses in the regime that gave Force a prime position. Force plays the role of an external shock, and, from a military point of view, technological advantages are always relative as the adversary adapts to the threat.

The traditional societies of India and China were non-egalitarian. The poor performance of the local administration when it came to crisis management has been observed over long historical periods. Demographic and economic regimes were better understood during the 20th Century. The unequal distribution of these macro-dynamic skills would play a significant role in the difference in levels of development. The tragedy of the Great Leap Forward and of the Cultural Revolution show how painful this learning of development could be.

1.3.3. *The consequences of global inequality*

The program set up by international organizations, focusing on point 3.8 in the SDG, is organized based on the type of health systems, classified according to the average income of each country. This takes into account existing inequalities between countries, and indeed, just as the inequality within countries has a structuring effect on health systems, so can the effect of external inequalities be demonstrated. By providing the Gini value (global inequality index) in econometric models, we can identify the characteristics of the performance of the health system on a global scale. In a way, there is thus a part-public part-private global health system with mediocre results in the prevention of early mortality, for example. This tends to diminish the share of non-reimbursed health expenses. Indeed, on a global scale, the Gini is very high, and there is no "global" middle class that can contribute to health expenses.

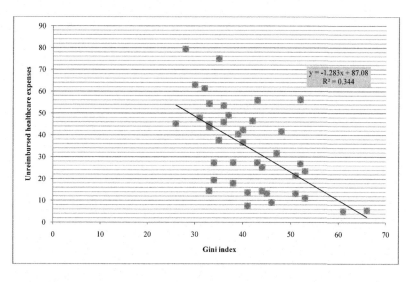

Figure 1.3. *An example of the calculation of the characteristic of the global health system using an inequality index (Gini)*

External resources (for countries with an annual per-head Purchasing Power Parity lower than $4,000) depend on global inequality and not internal inequality. Internal inequality (country-wise Gini index) is less influential in shaping health systems than global inequality. Countries with a high Gini index, mainly those in South America and Southern Africa, have, on average, a lower share of their GDP reserved for health and health systems and poorer performance of these health systems; however, their structures are not very different from the average global characteristics. The weakness of the middle class in these countries is correlated with a decrease in the share of unreimbursed healthcare costs. It is only the very poor countries that have a health system that is farthest from the characteristics of other countries in the world.

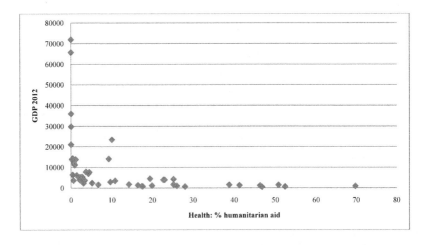

Figure 1.4. *Global inequality and humanitarian aid in health systems*

There are four broad types of health systems, namely: the Bismarck system (social rights for employees), the Beveridge system (parliamentary control on healthcare rights associated with citizenship), the "Alma-Alta" system (universal health coverage and care offered by health workers), and the "Humanitarian-Academic" system (healthcare supported by a training system). The first two systems, introduced toward the end of the 19th Century and the beginning of the 20th Century, were set up in a different context of inequality, though in societies that had completed their first industrialization. Thus, social security in Sweden was introduced to curb the massive emigration of Swedish workers to the United States in the first half of the 20th Century. The last two types of health system were introduced in the last 25 years of the 20th Century, in response to a situation where global inequality predominated. The sharp inequality in the world brought in the flow of international aid and measures put in place by intergovernmental agencies.

The more general underlying transformation is the transition of a society, which had nationally shared income from a primary sector (in this case, internal inequality was high, but there was little difference between the different societies) toward societies where these revenues were much smaller compared to revenue from industry and services. Health systems developed primarily in the second context.

1.4. On medical ethics

The oldest written expressions that we have for equity as a part of medical ethics are from the texts of the Indian medical system, "Ayurveda" (literally, knowledge of longevity). This is a written transcript of medical knowledge dating back to two millennia. A good doctor (*Vaidya*) treats all patients as if they were his own parents. However, medical knowledge was passed on through a guru–student tradition, which did not guarantee a stable level in the quality of care.

In Ancient Greece, the formulation of the Hippocratic oath is situated in a slightly more developed system of teaching. The student is asked to consider the doctor-teacher as a parent. This made it possible to widen recruitment for medical schools when a pandemic of malaria in that period caused a shortage of doctors.

The development of professional medical ethics in China led to a full treatise on this subject ("On the Absolute Sincerity of Great Physicians") by Sun Simiao, a Tao physician of the 7th Century AD. Under the Tang dynasty, a written exam became common practice in the teaching system. Medical students were asked to "work with the greatest attention" to minimize errors in future practice. For Sun Simiao, it was important that medicine be delivered with the aim of long life for all, not only for the emperor. He questioned the toxicity of treatments and criticized the vanity of the alchemists' pretensions. There is strong criticism of the slander between fellow doctors. Like Hippocrates, he prescribed diets that required the involvement of the patient.

There is a common factor in the expression of certain principles across these systems of medical ethics: benevolence; equity; contingent decisions; involvement of the patient and collaboration between colleagues; and striving for objectivity. Benevolence is defined by Mencius as "not seeking to harm"; Sun Simiao saw it as limiting therapeutics. Care must be extended to all. One of the topics discussed in the ancient Indian texts is related to the enemy: it is forbidden for the apprentices to care for the injured from the enemy army. The principle of individualizing treatment when necessary is discussed in the text "The Yellow Emperor", the most ancient text on Chinese medicine, which meets the ethics of the contingent decision-making process formulated in ancient Greek medicine. Reticence vis-à-vis one's colleagues was a source of concern shared by the different medical traditions. Objectivity of professional judgment is emphasized in Sun Simiao's treatise on ethics.

Integrated care only carries forward and updates some of these ethical principles. The main difference resides in a positive statement – be collaborative – a concern that has been of prime concern ever since the time of these ancient professional ethics texts: the exhortation to not have bad relations between fellow doctors. Do not harm – this also holds true for relations between colleagues, and it implies collaboration in the best interests of the patient.

2

Psychological and Social Factors of Health Inequalities

Although the persistence of inequality in healthcare has been well established, it has received no satisfactory explanation. Highly hierarchized societies have a decreasing life expectancy. Stress is the most commonly cited mechanism to explain this phenomenon [WIL 10]. However, the results of a study carried out in May 2008 in the Hauts-de-France region, in the north of France, suggest that there may be another explanation. The results showed that inequalities result in poor decision-making with respect to one's health, or personal, familial or medical decisions that have to do with prevention, the delay in turning to the health system, or the management of a treatment protocol. Some points of comparison make it possible to take into account this behavioral dimension when studying the question of global inequality, taking Morocco as the country of comparison, as it is the country with the median characteristics of all countries in the world.

Health inequalities bring about multiple determinants: living conditions, living habits, awareness about one's own health, organization of care, etc. Staggered life expectancies based on social position make up the "social gradient" puzzle: all other things being equal, a difference is observed between the life expectancy of a white-collar worker and a blue-collar laborer. Studies carried out in small territories show large differences in life expectancies: a difference of 17 years in the life expectancies for different neighborhoods in the same city (London), in a health system that was ranked 5th in the last global rankings published by *The Lancet*. In a French study carried out by regional health observatories, differences were observed between administrative districts that had comparable household income and that differed only in their relation to the health system based on more or less frequent visits to the hospital and other healthcare services. Other examples of research into the subtle determinants of inequality in health can be cited. Studies show that housing is a determinant in the social gradient; while housing conditions improved in the 1990s, the social gradient remained the same (data from France).

All the factors of inequality identified by epidemiological studies raise the following etiological question: how does a "macro"-social or -environmental characteristic manifest in the body and trigger a pathological process? The hypothesis of hierarchy of stress, where there are elevated stress levels lower down the social scale, has often been proposed to explain the social gradient. This explanation involves behavioral economics.

Behavioral economics emerged during a period when some health systems offered universal health coverage and when British epidemiologists realized that strong disparities persisted despite the fact that financial barrier limiting access to healthcare was no longer relevant. In behavioral economics, according to Puri and Robinson [PUR 07], it is possible to differentiate between "optimisms" that may alter the quality of the decision-making process applied by an individual with respect to their own health:

– "Absolute optimism", measured by the difference between declared life expectancy and actuarial life expectancy;

– "Social optimism", which is an overestimation of one's own abilities during a comparative evaluation, that is, judging yourself to be less weak or more competent than others, using an average individual as reference;

– "Professional optimism" or "field-wise optimism": for instance, a marine fisherman who declares that his profession is no more dangerous than any other, while objectively it is among the most dangerous professions.

The results of the study carried out in the Hauts-de-France region may be compared to similar studies carried out after Hurricane Katrina hit the United States. A high level of "absolute optimism" was observed among men, but not among women. There was a lot of procrastination before going in for care or preventative measures.

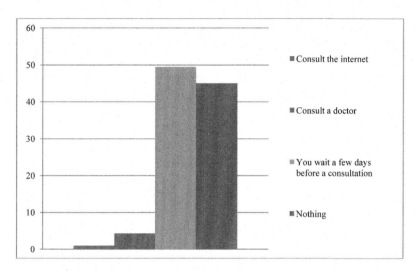

Figure 2.1. *"If you experience pain, what do you do first?" (Study by LEM, Hauts-de-France, 2008)*

One of the differences between the results of the Hauts-de-France study as compared with the American reference was low social optimism. Intense crises, which the sociologist Beck calls "emancipatory catastrophes", also mark the difference between regions that have been affected by them and by regions that have not experienced these crises. Hospital statistics show carbon monoxide (CO) poisoning and Legionnaires' disease in Moroccan hospitals, but there have been no public investigations into these issues.

The "hierarchic stress" hypothesis [WIL 10] is not very satisfactory in the case of the Hauts-de-France region. Involuntarily inactive individuals have the worst health, and they are not in a position of hierarchic subordination. The largest differences contrast the peri-urban residential zones of employees and the older, predominantly blue-collar worker residential zones. The proportion of superior professions is quite close here. The sample population chosen for the study was overexposed to risks. However, they cited certain habits as determining their state of health, and while measures were taken to face risks, this was only done partially and in a delayed manner. Among the people interviewed, illness was seen as "leisure time" (44%) and only 26% saw that it was a "major concern". Only 4% of those belonging to the sample of people who were strongly exposed to risk believed that "factors external to their habits" explained their state of health. A situation of overexposure indicated that other tasks displace adaptive measures from the order of priorities and erode their magnitude.

How do psychological factors increase health inequalities? According to Wilkinson's work [WIL 02, WIL 10], stress is the factor that is most often invoked. When in a hierarchic relation, the employees see their situation worsening with the stress they undergo. Our 2008 study focused on a region of France that used to have the best quality of healthcare and improvement in life expectancy before 1950. This result was from a "Bismarck" health system, where the health system was based on enterprise. For the first half of the 20th Century, companies in the industrial North offered their employees healthcare services. The fact that the company covered their employees' healthcare made it possible for this region to record a higher life expectancy than the rest of France, which was more rural at this time. The 2008 study shows a well-educated population, but one that has the lowest recourse to investigative medicine compared to the rest of France. Social transfers make up a large share of the revenue. Properties are smaller than in other places. These social inequalities seem amplified in the field of health. A part of the differential is seen in epidemics inherited from the grand industrial period, such as asbestosis and silicosis in former miners. However, this inherited morbidity as well as morbidity related to specific food habits is not enough to explain the disconnect in the region in terms of health.

The situation is one where there is a psychological reinforcement of the relatively low income from salary and income from property. Nonetheless, the psychosocial hypothesis of stress seems difficult to sustain. The Bismarck health system was one where hierarchy weighed heaviest. Present-day income transfers free up people from any hierarchic relation. The hierarchic stress hypothesis is, therefore, the reverse of the change observed in the Hauts-de-France region.

Health inequalities are often considered to be biological. In fact, inherited health is important for older people whose health will depend, above all, on their own biological history. However, there is a social dimension that explains the formation of "health-capital" over student life and professional life. France is among those European countries that have the highest levels of health inequality [MAC 08]. Indeed, public health experts state that the social inequalities in the field of health as well as mortality are rising. In 2000, given its performance, especially in terms of quality and equality of access to healthcare, the WHO placed France at the top of its world ranking. However, the gaps in health between social classes have deepened. This is seen on the one hand due to emerging pathologies (obesity) or chronic problems (disability) as well as in the field of mental health and on the other hand, when it comes to the prevention and screening of cardiovascular diseases and cancers. This persistence in health inequalities is also seen in the difference in life expectancies at birth.

In the first part of this chapter, we will present some theoretical results. In the second part, we will discuss important empirical results. Some points of comparison are provided with the situation in Morocco, in order to introduce a global behavioral perspective.

2.1. Approaches to studying inequality in health

In order to understand the determinants of the social inequalities of health, we will examine three approaches that shed light on the situation: the socioeconomic approach, the territorial approach, and the psychosocial and behavioral approach.

2.1.1. *Socioeconomic approach*

Public health indicators are less dependent on available medical services than on the socioeconomic conditions in which people live and work. Several researchers have shown that health inequalities are produced upstream of entry into the health system. The origins of social inequalities were, for a long time, explained by material living conditions. We talk of structural factors such as unemployment, poverty and work. How and why do these factors influence our health?

A strong correlation has often been observed between health problems and poverty, unemployment, housing, and food. Thus, people who live in absolute poverty have a higher risk of early death than those with higher incomes. Specialists speak of poverty-specific pathologies. Poverty has always been associated with unstable employment, low and unstable income from work, and the near-absence of income from inactivity (unemployment, illness, old age, etc.) [ABS 07]. Globalization, heightened competition and the advent of liberalized economies have led to an explosion in the informal economy and falling salaries, especially in developing countries, which has led to intense scrutiny on the subject of the conditions of wage-earners.

In fact, a lot of research on social inequalities related to health has centered on questions related to inequality in income and the fight against poverty. Inequalities in income from work, discrimination during hiring, and the inequality of access to the best-paid jobs explain a large part of inequality in employment. This leads to certain individuals getting locked into low-income jobs and persistent poverty.

Illnesses such as malnutrition, maternal mortality, AIDS, malaria, tuberculosis and diarrheal disorders often hit the poor. In other words, poverty engenders poor health by restricting access to medical care and health services. This can, of course, be explained by financial problems, but also by geographical and cultural difficulties that widen the gap between the health system and underprivileged individuals. Indeed, in addition to the gaps seen between socio-professional categories, inequalities are also explained by disparities that persist and increase between regions. In the face of these constraints, the most vulnerable population is more exposed to risks related to access to information and care and, consequently, to many illnesses. Social inequalities with respect to health are essentially the result or final product of other structural social inequalities in terms of resources, housing, food, employment and work, and schooling and training.

In the early 1980s, despite policies to improve working conditions and the considerable efforts taken to improve living conditions and equal access to care, there was an increase in social inequalities with respect to mortality in most countries. However, the publication of the Black report [BLA 82], led by Lord Black, strongly emphasized the fact that the socioeconomic gradient for health appeared to be a reflection of social inequalities rather than of individual differences. In fact, social inequalities cannot be reduced to a distinction between rich and poor, nor can they be explained only by living conditions. One of the hypotheses that the report underlined was "the selection effect", which suggested that inequality in mortality rates may not be the result of the impact of social status on health, but on the contrary, the result health has on social status and social mobility [COU 05]. The impact of health on the risk of job loss and, conversely, the effect of unemployment on health is a matter of intense debate even today.

2.1.2. Geographic disparities and social inequalities in health

Many researchers have explored the relationship between the location and the effects of food practices on health. For example, it was observed in the United States that residential neighborhoods and food habits are related: supermarkets in the most upmarket neighborhoods offered the widest variety of food. However, this was not seen in poorer neighborhoods, which were characterized by food that was less healthy. Anna Diez-Roux [DIE 01] specifies that in poorer neighborhoods, it is easier to find tobacco than healthy food. According to experts, this strong relationship between one's neighborhood and nutritional behavior explains to a great extent the variability in the incidence of diabetes. Thus, health inequalities weigh especially heavily on populations that live in neighborhoods or localities that have strong social and economic disadvantages. As a result, territorial inequalities partly explain social inequalities in health.

This discovery is in line with the results obtained on social health inequalities by the Regional Health Observatories in France. Indeed, a study showed that the prevalence of childhood obesity is greater among the children of blue-collar workers who are educated in sensitive zones. In addition to obesity problems, these "priority education zones"[1] are characterized by the presence of children who suffer from visual problems and untreated tooth decay. Other studies in these areas highlight the existence of problems related to the early onset of certain illnesses such as cancer. In fact, a study carried out by regional health observatories observed regional inequality with respect to risky behavior and illness. Indeed, there is greater inequality in mortality following cancer when there is an increase in territorial inequalities. This observation has been confirmed by risk levels, which are twice as high in cases where there is no gynecological follow-up, especially in underprivileged zones. These inequalities are observed even within the same *Départment* (French administrative region) where the population of certain sectors is in good health, while just a few kilometers away, there are sectors where the population suffers from poor health. The High Committee for Public Health drew attention to the large regional disparity in health conditions among the French. Even so, mortality rates are variable according to the regional North/South disparity. The study, which was based on a population in the age range 15–29 years, highlighted the degree-of-urbanization hypothesis that suggests that the North of France, which is heavily urbanized, is characterized by an under-mortality, while rural Bretagne is marked by an over-mortality among people of this age group. Another explanation for the territorial gradient resides in region-specific food habits (cooking with butter and beer, animal fat, olive oil, etc.). Different studies have shown that there is excessive consumption of alcohol in the *Départements* of the North and in Bretagne. This is an important explanation for geographical disparities in premature mortality linked to alcoholism.

---

1 Priority Education Zones (*Zones d'éducation prioritaire*) were created in France in 1982 to provide additional resources and opportunities to schools in disadvantaged areas.

In 2007, the inequalities observatory noted that from the age of six years onwards, there were significant differences in obesity and tooth decay, especially among marginalized populations. These problems, which have an early onset and which are combined with unstable social situations, are indicators of serious cardiovascular problems in adulthood. Indeed, the difficulties faced by underprivileged populations are reflected in their food habits. A number of studies have associated malnutrition and diabetes with the social situation and geographic origins of individuals. Chauvin and Parizot [CHA 05] observed a relationship between social inequalities linked to food habits on the one hand, and socioeconomic conditions and psychosocial and territorial parameters on the other.

A lot of research has been carried out on the long-term determinants of the increase in obesity all over the world. If we explain this by technological changes (industrial jobs have disappeared, replaced by work that does not require intense physical activity), obesity would be seen only in "postindustrial" societies. However, it also affects underdeveloped or developing countries [PHI 03]. Explanations that refer to the change in the food available (the introduction of fast food restaurants) cannot take into account a decrease of physical activity [PHI 01]. According to the Philipson and Posner model, obesity should stop increasing once industrial transformation is complete. This plateau-effect has not been observed and would have indicated a collective learning of technological risks. The long-term data on obesity treat it as a "natural risk" and not as a transient risk based on poorly adapted behavior, which will disappear over time. This leads us to also consider non-behavioral factors. The article by Leung Chi et al. [LEU 07] on "Lower Risk of Tuberculosis in Obesity" introduces a new perspective on the determinants for the increase in the prevalence of obesity. They used a Chinese database with an incidence rate for tuberculosis of 90 per 100,000 (the rate is lower than 9 per 100,000 in France, but higher than 300 for a much poorer country like Haiti). Malnutrition (two-thirds of Haiti's population) is associated with tuberculosis (for example, a prevalence of 306 per 100,000 in Haiti). Excess weight in older people reduces the risk of pulmonary tuberculosis. Given a "toxic" environment, being overweight might be a survival strategy. There are also overweight people in Haiti, but below the global average. Social inequalities and an association of pathologies thus create complex dynamics.

2.1.3. *Psychosocial and behavioral approach*

Social inequalities in health are not explained exclusively by material and biological factors, but also by psychosocial mechanisms [MAR 99].

Research carried out on factors determining social health inequalities focused on living conditions, work and loss of employment, while psychosocial factors were marginalized. However, experts began to change their perspective to also include psychosocial factors that may have an impact on health.

Studies carried out on the effects of mourning show that the death of a spouse increases the risk of premature death of the surviving partner [WIL 02]. However, it cannot be deduced from this that psychosocial factors constitute one of the main causes of social inequality where health is concerned. Indeed, health is highly dependent on living conditions and life history. Today, a number of studies on the hardships that an individual undergoes in life (such as resettling, divorce, loss of employment, a loved one falling seriously ill, being obliged to change professions, etc.) have confirmed their negative influence on health. Researchers estimate that the psychological states associated with upsets in life must also be interpreted as warning signs. The stressful nature of these difficult times produces harmful effects either directly (causing physiological excitations that could be damaging to one's health by transforming chronic anxiety into a real pathology) or indirectly (with the appearance of behavior that is harmful to health, such as smoking, as a response to stress).

The biologist Robert Sapolsky [SAP 98] explains the chain of biological mechanisms stimulated by anxiety and physiological excitation that destabilize the control system and weaken the defenses of the organism, its immune system, and its ability to resist multiple pathogenic situations. Indeed, when stress is perceived, the organism reacts to this danger by releasing adrenalin and cortisol, insulin, and other hormones whose purpose is to allow the organism to instantly make use of energy instead of storing it for the future. Short-term stress has a stimulating effect on the immune system, but if the stress persists, it significantly weakens the organism's defenses and provokes pathologies (hypertension, cardiovascular illnesses) that result from the unnecessary stimulation of the defense mechanisms. The appearance of the pathogenic effects of chronic anxiety also contributes to the socioeconomic gradient and the influence that the psychosocial mechanisms have on health.

Work and unemployment can both have a negative impact on one's health. The relationship between working conditions and health problems is seen repeatedly in international or national studies. Indeed, poor working conditions are the causes not only for accidents but for the physical and mental wear and tear of an individual. Poor working conditions mainly affect laborers and workers, rather than the management and the people working in intermediate professions. Not only are the lives of the blue-collar workers shorter than those of people working in management or other positions, but they also live with incapacitating conditions for longer than them [CAM 08]. Some categories of workers and laborers suffer from muscular-skeletal problems, which are a result of repetitive work. Similarly, the intensity of work and new forms of organization of work, especially the introduction of new information communication techniques, are a source of stress and mental exhaustion among management.

Many studies have shown that frequency of unemployment and job insecurity is very unequally distributed between social categories. Broadly speaking, it is four times higher among unqualified workers than among management. Indeed, the link between the loss of employment and health has pushed researchers to recognize that either layoffs considerably weaken a person's health, or people with weaker health are the majority of those laid-off. Studies carried out on factories closing following collective layoffs (the state of health of the employee is not taken into account) have renewed the debate on pathologies among the unemployed. The results have shown that not only does unemployment result in a deterioration of the individual's health condition, but the threat of layoffs and the fear of losing employment also results in the weakening of physical resistance. This discovery confirms that the role of psychosocial processes on the social gradient for health cannot be neglected.

2.2. Risky behavior and health inequalities

The question of personal responsibility for the deterioration or preservation of one's own health has long been debated. Today, it is impossible to deny the negative effects that pathogenic behaviors (tobacco use, alcoholism, a sedentary life) have on one's health. The excessive consumption of tobacco or alcohol, the quality of education that children receive, nutrition, physical exercise and drug use – all of these contribute significantly to social inequalities related to health. However, they are far from explaining the magnitude of the inequalities.

Studies in Great Britain (which has a highly developed social epidemiology) have shown that the majority of these inequalities are not consequences of the behavior of "at risk" individuals and must be viewed in a global manner. Most of the activities undertaken by humans have some element of risk. This risk may have an impact on the physical or mental wellbeing of a person, to a lesser or greater degree, and in material or financial terms. Indeed, risk taking results from two phenomena: an individual takes risks because it strongly enhances the satisfaction derived from the risky activity and/or because the individual is an optimist or negligent of the risk involved.

An individual who takes risks for him/herself also puts other at risks. This may generate strong external negatives, which is especially the case on the road. Poor risk perception also comes into play in material terms where excessive optimism may result in ill-considered investments. Thus, taking individual risks today can sometimes cause major losses both for an individual and for the society, which must consent to large public spending to meet these losses and suffers human loss, which is both economically as well as socially expensive. Attitudes toward risks differ depending on the subjects and age. However, individuals can make such a decision using the information available to them and taking help from others.

When examining the risk of pathogenic behaviors, we ask the following questions: why do these individuals engage in risky activities? How do they perceive and evaluate these risks? Why are certain risks systematically overestimated and others underestimated?

2.2.1. Optimism, risk and health inequalities

At the decisional level, risk taking assumes the existence of a risk in the broad sense, that is, a hazard. When this hazard is unknown, we speak of ambiguity or even of uncertainty when there is total ignorance of the hazard [CAM 92]. If we better understand the behaviors deployed in risky situations as well as the underlying psychological mechanisms, we can then try to prevent risky behaviors and restore social optimum. There is, in fact, an interaction between our psychological, biological and behavioral characteristics and the functioning of the society in which we evolve.

Risk is a multidimensional concept that incorporates factors such as uncertainty, fear, catastrophic potential, controllability and familiarity, all of which will vary depending on the characteristics of those evaluating the situation (beliefs, culture, social position, age, sex, etc.) [KOU 06].

A large section of literature focuses on the study of individual rationality and behavior. On the one hand, in order to understand whether there is a relation between the rational model and human behavior, psychologists attempt to define how individuals make choices and really make decisions. On the other hand, sociology has introduced a social dimension to explain risky behaviors. Sociology considers that risk is endogenous to contemporary societies as, very often, the risk arises from living conditions and social pressure.

2.2.2. *Risk perception and health inequalities*

Behavior is not linear and individuals react depending on the need for cognitive consistency and on the basis of their representations and experiences. Many studies have shown that on the one hand, behavior is influenced by knowledge, beliefs and attitudes, while on the other hand, adopting a given behavior may in turn influence an individual's attitudes, representations and beliefs [FES 64, KRU 66, VAU 80]. However, many empirical studies have also shown that the diffusion of knowledge does not automatically lead to the modification of risky behaviors (alcoholism, tobacco use, AIDS, etc.). Prevention campaigns help to make people aware of the risk they run and enhance their knowledge, but they have very little actual influence on the behavior of individuals.

This means that improved knowledge on means of prevention and control is not enough to lead to an improvement in individual behavior [MOA 93]. Indeed, the gap between recommendations and practice do not always seem related to a lack of knowledge, and there are other psychological and sociological factors that make it possible to explain this gap.

In utilitarian logic, individual behavior is based on economic rationality – on the relationship between ends and means – and consequently, a person carries out rational calculations of costs/benefits when taking each decision. Simon [SIM 55, SIM 79, SIM 91] uses cognitive psychology and the observation of decision-making processes to propose a radical revision of the analysis of economic behaviors.

"In a wider definition of rationality, practically any human behavior is rational. People have reasons for doing what they do and, if we ask them about it, they can give their opinions as to what these reasons are" [SIM 91, p. 1]. According to the author, rationality is limited because these individuals commit errors of judgment and do not always reach the goals they set. Given the importance of hazards and uncertainty in the environment of individual and collective choices, we are witnessing a new approach to the concept of risk by researchers that challenge the classical paradigm of the expectation of utility proposed by Daniel Bernoulli and taken up by John Von

Neumann. This model assumes that agents seek to maximize their expectation of future happiness based on a distribution of objective or subjective probability of future events. This happiness, according to the author, is an increasing function of prosperity: the richer one is, the lower the increase is in happiness upon a given increase in this wealth. This model, which made it possible to explain qualitative phenomena, failed to explain in quantitative areas, a large number of observed paradoxes in behavior when faced with a risk. This led two psychologists, Tversky and Kahneman [KAH 92], to construct an alternative model by introducing a cognitive dimension to behavioral economics.

2.2.3. The psychosocial approach and risky behaviors

Work carried out in social and cognitive psychology shows that behavior is complex, and that the rationality of agents is fundamentally limited by their own abilities and the features of the economic universe (informational asymmetries, radical uncertainty); consequently, an individual does not seek an optimal solution, but a satisfactory solution [SIM 55, CRO 77]. Given this limited rationality and the significant cost in terms of money and time of the individual choice process, a person has limited calculation abilities and takes a decision that they judge to be satisfactory based on their own perception of reality.

The research program carried out in social and cognitive psychology has highlighted a set of cognitive rules and heuristic strategies that an individual employs in order to evaluate and make a choice. According to Kahneman and Tversky, in a situation of uncertainty, people develop their judgments based on heuristics, which can often be useful, but can also lead to biases. Both authors define heuristics as being short and approximate judgments that replace long reasoning or a statistical observation when explaining an event [KAH 82]. According to this theory, the individual can incorporate a pessimistic concept and associate preferences and beliefs when making a decision. The individual can also incorporate into his preferences the need to transform the objective distribution of probabilities in favor of the states that are the least favorable for him.

People have a tendency to measure their wellbeing not in absolutes, but with relation to others. The risks taken by other people play a driving role in the risk taken by the individual. In theory, we consider that if a risk is acceptable for each member of a society, it is then "socially acceptable". Psychologists have noted that in the perception and evaluation of risks, behaviors are not dictated by facts, but by representations of these facts. In a probabilistic vision of risk, we speak of the objective probability of an event that represents either the true probability value or an estimation that is based on the past observation of similar events. On the other hand, we have a subjective probability that arises from beliefs or judgments and represents a value constructed by thought. In this case, the subjective representation of risk is highly affectively charged and brings up feelings of uncertainty and insecurity that people may dwell on, even though actual insecurities might have little effect on them. According to Kahneman and Tversky, the evaluation of risk by agents is a contingent process. The heuristics that they display are convenient, but result in bias when estimating a situation.

Kahneman and Tversky [KAH 82, KAH 96] identified three broad types of heuristics: representativeness, availability, and anchorage and adjustment. Representativeness is when an individual analyzes a risk situation based on the situations experienced earlier. The use of this heuristic leads to biases, that is, systematic errors in judgment and decision-making. The availability heuristic is when a person uses the most publicized and recent information available to evaluate the risk. This also leads to biases in judgment. Finally, the anchoring and adjustment heuristic is when the individual uses a past event as a reference point (anchor) to adjust and represent the current situation. This shows that an agent forms their beliefs based on the different risks that they face and based on the information at their disposal. In order to do this, the individual often takes recourse to their social environment and their personal history. Risk evaluation is thus based on the alchemy between personal functioning and the functioning of the environment in which the individual lives. When people have very little information available, their perceptions are the result of their general preferences [GAN 06].

Risk is also measured by its frequency and seriousness: a risk perceived as being serious leads to a change in behavior and attitudes toward health. In fact, the characteristics of a risk determine the degree of perceived seriousness: a risk that is seen as familiar, voluntary, generalized or of natural origins is seen as weak. An involuntary or unfamiliar risk or one that has human origins is seen as more serious. Apart from the characteristics of the risk, studies highlight psychological characteristics that make an individual decide whether or not taking a risk is favorable. The perceived degree of risk is determined by a mixture of professional knowledge and beliefs and conceptions that are shared by one's network.

2.3. Optimism and risk perception

Many studies have shown that people differ in how they evaluate a risk for themselves or for loved ones and how they evaluate a risk for the general population. They systematically estimate themselves as being less exposed to risk compared to others. In fact, the underestimation of certain risks is seen as a form of optimism, which goes back to the comparison between the anticipation of positive events and the anticipation of negative events. Researchers speak of "unrealistic optimism" [WEI 80, LEE 95], "the optimism bias", and even sometimes of "comparative unrealistic optimism" [WEI 95]. Weinstein defines optimism as the continued practice of unhealthy behaviors, linked to inadequate risk perception and unrealistic optimism. Comparative optimism is measured by the comparison between oneself and others: it is the general tendency to see the future more favorably for oneself than for others. Indeed, studies carried out on the perception of the risk of exposure to more or less frequent illnesses show that each person thought they would be likelier to escape the risk than other people. Weinstein [WEI 80] describes four cognitive factors that contribute to unrealistic optimism: a lack of personal experience with the problem, the belief that the problem may be avoided by an action taken by the person, the belief that if the problem has not come up so far it will not come up in the future, and finally, the belief that the problem is not very common. These factors suggest that the perception of risks for oneself is not a rational process.

Ambroise Paré, a 16th-Century French physician, recounts the following anecdote in his treatise on medicine: during a journey, he had a bad fall from a horse and sustained an open fracture and other complications. In his professional practice, Paré had reintroduced the practice of amputation for injuries with poor prognosis due to gangrene caused by firearms – or falls from a horse. However, with the help of an assistant trained in surgery, he managed to save his own leg – contrary to the protocol that the treatise recommended, showing opportunism in taking the medical decision and a certain amount of unrealistic optimism.

Heaton [HEA 95] studied the relationship between risk perception and excessive confidence through a study on the optimism of managers. This research shows that overinvestment and underinvestment result from managerial optimism. In fact, errors in perception of the cash flow generated by projects bring about an overestimation of investment opportunities, which leads managers to take greater risks. These studies confirmed that those with the most excessive confidence were those who invested the most in risky portfolios. Several authors have shown that a person may be pessimistic about absolute value and yet be optimistic when comparing themselves to others [VAN 92]. To explain this tendency, other authors adopt the terms bias or error. They estimate that an individual is "mistaken" compared to a reality that can be virtually quantified. Optimism is a phenomenon that is over-determined by many cultural, cognitive and motivational factors.

2.3.1. *Optimism in the motivational approach*

Authors who defend the motivational approach adopt the self-defense hypothesis, where a person is motivated by the goal of psychological wellbeing and reduction of anxiety. Indeed, in order to enhance their self-esteem and maintain their personal identity, people are likely to skew the distribution of positive and negative events to favor themselves. Thus, Peeters, Cammaert and Czapinski [PEE 97] defend the idea that comparative optimism is adapted to an environment where negative events are more frequent than positive events. Empirical studies have shown that people are not particularly optimistic with respect to others when they do not feel that they can control the events that occur (such as a natural catastrophe). On the other hand, based on the information available on the behavior of others, an individual can adjust the perceptions of their own engagement in risky behaviors. According to the theory of positive illusion proposed by Taylor and Brown [TAY 88], individuals dupe themselves in order to retain positive humor and to interact positively with others. The authors state that three illusions guarantee good psychological health: an unrealistically positive perception of the self, the illusion of control, and optimism.

In literature on optimism, reducing anxiety is often cited as another motivation for optimism. The future is a source of anxiety due to the uncertainty associated with it, and in order to fight this anxiety, people anticipate a future in which negative events will be rare and positive events frequent.

A study carried out by Taylor *et al.* [TAY 92] shows that while optimism is a defense mechanism against anxiety, anxious people defend themselves the least. Other authors [NOR 86, SHO 92] show that the battle against anxiety is often carried out through pessimism rather than through optimism.

2.3.2. *Optimism according to the cognitive approach*

According to cognitive explanations, several factors lead to the emergence of optimism, but the majority of authors subordinate this phenomenon to "errors" during social comparison, by either underestimating the risk for oneself or by overestimating it for others. In fact, literature on cognitive factors for optimism defines four categories of positive biases: information gathering errors and contingent judgments, positivity of persons, egocentrism and downward comparisons. Indeed, the reliability of comparative judgments depends on information that the individual retains from among all the information that comes to them [LEE 95]. According to these authors, even when informed, the individual may commit errors in contingent judgments. It is therefore necessary to examine the mechanisms of information processing and to take into account these processes during a comparative judgment. Another hypothesis regarding the positivity of people was postulated concerning errors that may be committed by the individual. A lot of research [HAR 94, PER 86] shows that optimism is lower when the individual compares themselves to a friend or a loved one rather than with a stranger. However, these individuals have complex cognitive and affective representations for their loved ones, which they do not have with respect to a stranger [KIH 84].

Weinstein [WEI 80] suggests that egocentrism is another factor that contributes to the emergence of optimism. Individuals have a tendency to think that they are the only ones to adopt safe behavior, as they know the pros and cons of a future event. However, they do not have adequate information regarding the behavior of others vis-à-vis a risk.

Finally, downward comparison, which some authors associate with a cognitive mechanism, means that people apply a representativeness heuristic [KAH 83]; using this heuristic, they deploy a stereotype to which they have attributed the characteristics of a person at risk, and they imagine that there is little chance that this bears any resemblance to themselves. For the same category of illness, the individual estimates that others are systematically less careful than themselves, and that they themselves are thus in less danger than others.

Literature on optimism has allowed us to consider this phenomenon as arising above all from a situation of social comparison. In fact, both motivational and cognitive explanations, together or separately, contribute to detachment or rapprochement between the self and the others in terms of risk perception and the adoption of a pathogenic behavior.

The study "Optimism and inequality" clearly highlights two points: the marked character of social optimism in the case studies carried out based on data collected in the United States, and the existence of an absolute optimism among men, independent of any social comparison. The mobilization of different theoretical contributions has allowed us to construct a reading grid that makes it possible to take into account variability, the definition, and the measurement of optimism. These theoretical findings seemed particularly promising in shedding new light on the hypothesis that psychological phenomena reinforce and deepen health inequalities. In order to verify the pertinence of these hypotheses, we carried out an empirical study in May 2008 in the Hauts-de-France region, using a cluster survey.

2.4. The study: methodology and data collection

A study was carried out in May 2008 among 300 people in the Hauts-de-France region, in clusters of people exposed to pathogenic environments, using questionnaires comprising a general section and a separate section specific to each group, concerning the particular situation of the population being studied. It would be rather absurd to ask everyone in the population questions about using pesticides in an open field, whereas it makes perfect sense to ask farmers about it. The results of these specific questionnaires were published as monographs.

The study covered five zones in the Hauts-de-France region (in the north of France). We wished to study certain psychosocial aspects that would make it possible to identify the presence of risky behaviors, which explain health inequalities.

In the Arrageois basin, the study focused on the risk of pesticide poisoning that the farmers faced. This was a priority issue, as studies carried out among people from many different populations show that pesticides have a significant impact on health: disorders of the central nervous system, cognitive disorders (memory, attention), degenerative diseases (for example, Parkinson's and Alzheimer's), cancer, and reproductive disorders (sterility, deformations). The incidence of Parkinson's was five times higher among workers who used pesticide, as compared to the general population, and the incidence of Alzheimer's was 2.4 times higher. There is not enough epidemiological, toxicological or biological data to allow for rapid progress in our knowledge of the health impact of pesticides, but studies have been carried out to demonstrate the risks involved with using these products. Inasmuch as workers in this sector have efficient protective measures available to them (such as gloves, protective suits, respiratory masks), the motivations that lead them to use or not make use of these protective devices must be studied.

As regards the Béthune basin, we questioned 84 individuals with the aim of understanding the relationship between behavior and the risk of CO poisoning. In the Lille region, we studied pollution by tropospheric ozone, and for the Saint-Omer region, we studied the risk of flooding.

Finally, there are three types of risk of exposure to and contamination by legionella. The first is a hospital-acquired infection following a period of hospitalization. This was not of interest to the study. The second is industrial risk, when legionella bacteria escape from air-cooler towers, vehicle washing stations, etc. The third and final case is individual contamination, following the growth of legionella bacteria in hot water networks. We have sought to measure risk perception and identify the preventive measures taken after an epidemic episode of Legionnaires' disease.

Our study is divided into three sections. We first list the information on the individuals relative to the risk faced (flooding, CO poisoning, ozone pollution, legionella contamination, and poisoning through agrochemical products). We then examine their exposure to these risks, and finally, we study the predispositions relative to taking preventive measures vis-à-vis the risk. We will examine each of these below.

2.4.1. *Information on those surveyed vis-à-vis the risk*

Let us begin with agrochemical products. These products are used most often by farmers; however, using them is not without consequence. While farmers generally think that organic farming makes it possible to protect nature, paradoxically only 20 of them (35.7%) felt threatened by different kinds of poisoning. We note that all, or almost all, the farmers who participated in the study used fungicides, herbicides, insecticides and growth regulators. All of them knew that the storage of products of this type is regulated. Therefore, this leads us to think that they are relatively ill-informed of the risks that they run in using these agrochemical products. Moving on to the user manuals for agrochemical products: 93% of farmers confirmed that their products were delivered with user manuals, while others seemed ready to ask for them. We can therefore conclude that they generally have satisfactory access to the list of precautions to take when using these products. However, many farmers mix products before spraying them, even though the chemical reactions that result from this mixing have not been scientifically studied. Farmers do not, therefore, have access to the recommendations for this type of handling. Additionally, when farmers fall ill, 7% of them go straightway to the doctor, while the others prefer to wait to get better or wait for several days before visiting the doctor. This leads us to think that farmers have relatively negligent behavior vis-à-vis illness, but are less negligent than the average population. Other individual variables, such as age, socio-professional origins and the level of education, are intuitively fundamental in explaining these professional behaviors in a field where handling dangerous products is quite common.

As concerns questions related to the risk of CO poisoning, we observe that only 45 out of 82 individuals say they were informed by the Directorate of Health and Social Affairs for the *Départment*, the Regional Directorate of Health and Social Affairs as well as the Poison Control Centre or another organization. One piece of information that seems important to us is knowing whether the person surveyed personally knows any victim or victims of CO poisoning. Of the 77 respondents to this question, 47 replied "No", while 30 said "Yes" (25 of these were victims of malfunctions in a coal-heating system or a badly cleaned chimney). It seems valid to assume that, all other things being equal, a person who knows about a case of poisoning will be more careful about implementing protective means against CO poisoning.

Finally, as concerns the risk of legionella contaminations in an automobile washing station or in a swimming pool, 27 (36%) and 44 (59%), respectively, of those questioned thought they were exposed to the risk, which is relatively low, given that this is indeed a real risk (two examples: infections from a Strasbourg swimming pool, and a Lyon car-washing center at the time of the study). On the other hand, 44 (59%) of those questioned thought that drinking tap-water may lead to contamination, which is scientifically false. Within our sample of 74 individuals, no one knew or had themselves been a victim of

Legionnaires' disease. However, 63 (85%) estimated that this was a serious illness. Within the context of this study, we asked questions about the NOROXO affair, which took place in 2003–2004, in order to characterize the information that the people we interviewed possessed concerning the risk. Only 32% of the respondents stated that they did not know about this matter, while among the 50 other individuals who were better informed, only 3 emphasized that their behavior had been modified by this, and thought that this kind of an epidemic could be repeated and that this worried them. However, it is important to underline that half of the 74 respondents estimated that they were not predisposed to contract the illness either because they were in good health (16 people) or because their general living conditions were good (21 people). Finally, 29 people (39%) responded that they did not know.

2.4.2. Risk perception

As regards the perception of risk of poisoning in the course of their professional activities, we observed that the more people thought that they were in good health, the more they tended to underestimate the risk. Thus, a farmer who estimates that he is in perfect health, sees illness as just a transient phase, or a farmer who works on a large scale, estimates his risk of poisoning to be 2.24 out of 10. We can see that the average score for the combined population is 5.87. As concerns the problem of storing agrochemical products, 19 out of the 56 farmers stated that they had already encountered such a problem. All the same, it seems that the most highly educated of them are less likely to suffer these problems than the others.

In fact, 46 out of 56 farmers affirmed that they had been exposed to the risk of absorption of toxic products through respiration. Just being in possession of a list of substances that could lead to poisoning seems to (positively) explain this fear. We can then conjecture that individuals who do not possess this list are unaware of the risk of inhaling substances that could damage their health. We observed that on the one hand, 39 out of 56 agreed that they were exposed to the risk of absorption of toxic substances through skin. The fact of having already been poisoned seems especially to (positively) explain this feeling. On the other hand, 35 farmers felt that they were exposed to the risk of oral absorption of toxic products. Being well-informed about the risk of pneumopathy as well as the fact of using agrochemical products more than once a month seems to have a positive effect on this variable. As concerns lung cancers or leukemia, farmers do not think that they are particularly more exposed to this than the rest of the population of France.

We observed that compared to women, men and older persons are more "optimistic" about the probability of catching Legionnaires' disease. This is because they underestimate the probability of catching the illness, which results in a certain form of social inequality due to the optimism bias. We see that in fact people with lower incomes (monthly income lower than 700 euros) consider that they are less exposed to the risk of contracting Legionnaires' disease. This is a perfect example of an optimism bias inherent to a form of economic inequality. Finally, it was found that people who considered illnesses "in general" to be a passing phase in their life, rather than a hindrance to their work or a major concern, also estimated themselves to be less exposed to the risk of contracting Legionnaires' disease. This again gives us an example of optimism bias, one that is neither social nor economic, but a psychological one.

Inasmuch as the majority of CO poisoning cases have involved heating systems, we studied the type of heating used by the respondents in the study: 46 out of 80 had gas heating, 15 had electrical heating systems, 12 had oil-fired heating systems, 5 had wood-burning systems, 2 had coal-based heating systems and 1 person used a different form of heating. Twenty-four had heating systems that had been installed in the past 3 years, 21 had heating systems between 3 and 5 years old, 17 had heating systems that were 5–10 years old, and 20 had heating systems older than 10 years. Out of the 82 people who were interviewed, 18 had equipment such as a barbecue or a brazier that was operated within their residence.

2.4.3. *Preventative measures vis-à-vis risk*

When studying the preventive behaviors adopted vis-à-vis the risk of CO poisoning, it was seen that individuals are characterized by a certain number of important variables. When we asked the people interviewed if they could implement measures to prevent CO poisoning, 42% responded in the affirmative. Among the 41 respondents who said "No", 18 indicated that this was because they did not know about such measures, 6 said it was because they were very expensive and 17 people had other reasons. However, the fact of having followed a specific training program on risks and health, being a landowner as well as being a smoker who was trying to quit – all had a positive influence on the probability of their possessing a controlled mechanical ventilation (CMV). It must be pointed out that knowing someone who had been the victim of CO poisoning had a positive impact on the adoption of behaviors to prevent this, while people with children were also better informed on the means of prevention against CO poisoning.

As concerns the risk of using agrochemical products, prevention is dependent on the knowledge of the product, the application protocol and the wearing of individual protective equipment. In our study, we divided these means of prevention into regular medical exams and means of protection that can be used every day by farmers in the course of their daily activities. Twenty out of 56 farmers have a health check-up at least once every two years, compared to 36 who go less often. Thirty-one have medical tests done at least once every two years. Age and education levels are the variables that have a favorable impact on the frequency of the medical tests. As regards the means of protection made available to farmers for use during their professional activities, 46 out of the 56 farmers interviewed used gloves as a means of protection. We found that farmers working on large-scale production, who had a good level of education and who used agrochemical products intensively, used a protective suit. Only 25 of the 56 wore protective goggles, and 39 confirmed that they used a mask. We noted that age also had a positive impact on this behavior.

When we study the behavior of people vis-à-vis the risk of a Legionnaires' epidemic, we see that on the one hand, the more people consider themselves to be in good health, the less ready they are to adopt preventive measures against an epidemic at the community level. On the other hand, 20 out of 56 respondents said that they would do nothing because they did not know what measures to adopt. Older people, smokers, tenants, those with a monthly income lower than 700 euros and those who saw illness as a passing phase were in this category.

This study allowed us to observe that there was an "optimism bias" that covered economic, sociological as well as psychological factors. The farmers interviewed practiced intensive agriculture, with daily use of agrochemical products sprayed by tractor. However, while 93% of these farmers confirmed that they had information on the use of their agrochemical products, many of them mixed products without the potential harmful effects of these mixtures having been scientifically studied. About one-third of them had already encountered problems with the storage of their products. It also seems here that the less educated among them were more often the victims than the others.

Even though the people had the necessary information available, we saw a gap between the knowledge of recommended behavior and the practices actually carried out. Consequently, they exposed themselves to the risk of CO poisoning, agrochemical product poisoning or contamination by legionella.

This discrepancy can be explained, on the one hand, by economic determinants, (characterized by the low financial resources of these individuals) and on the other hand, by psychological factors that signify that a person's behavior is limited by their individual perception of reality. This leads people to associate preferences and beliefs and bring in an optimistic perspective when taking a decision, which makes it possible to commit errors in judgments and pushes a person to adopt risky behavior.

Finally, we have sociocultural determinants that are defined by the pressure exerted by society and one's living environment. This is confirmed by the accounts the farmers give of their working conditions: as this profession is highly dependent on climatic conditions, they must make the best use of the favorable conditions, at harvest time, for example. The specific demands of this profession, coupled with the current problems faced by farmers vis-à-vis intensive cultivation, as well as the downward pressure on their operating profits lead to the farmers sometimes being obliged to give up precautionary measures when using agricultural products. For example, not wearing gloves or protective suits, which reduces their productivity, or ignoring the recommendation to not use the products on windy days.

When it comes to the perceived state of health, it seems that the fact of not living on an agricultural land, possessing a list of the substances that carry the risk of poisoning, or of not feeling that one is exposed to the risk of absorbing toxic products through respiration or the skin, all have a favorable impact on the perceived state of health. We observed that there is an optimism bias regarding risk perception. In fact, the degree of risk perception is determined by a mixture of professional knowledge and beliefs and conceptions shared in one's networks. A person systematically estimates that they are less exposed to risk compared to other people. In fact, the underestimation of certain risks shows that optimism is a defense mechanism against anxiety in an environment where negative events are more frequent than positive events. Thus, an individual has a tendency to think that they are better informed than others, and consequently, that they are the only ones who adopt precautionary measures (egocentrism).

When it comes to the risk of legionella contamination, we can clearly see that on the one hand, individuals who know about the Noroxo incident are more likely to fear a similar episode recurring, and on the other hand, the risk of catching Legionnaires' disease at an automobile washing station or in a pool is relatively high. It is important to note that when a person knows of a case of poisoning, they become more careful about taking measures to protect against CO poisoning. Indeed, depending on the information available to them about the behavior that others adopt, the individual adjusts their perception of their own engagement in risky behaviors.

The gap seen between the perception of information on a risk and the adoption of risky behaviors does not always seem linked to a lack of knowledge and seems to be explained by other psychological and sociocultural factors. The fact that farmers are able to recognize the problem shows that not conforming to recommendations is not a problem related to the perception of real risks. The gap between theory and practice can be explained by failure in communication and especially by poorly identifying the target population. In fact, we saw that it was mainly poorer and less educated people who were most exposed to different risks. We can say that information on risks does not take into account individual and social representations, nor the psychological and sociological determinants of behavior. This leads to differences in risk perception and evaluation between the agents responsible for communication and the public receiving the information. Public authorities must inform, educate and sensitize people to risk levels and give them information for knowledge and judgment, both to increase their awareness and diminish their concerns, as well as to reinforce their abilities to make choices and take decisions relative to their health.

2.4.4. Ozone pollution among the well-off in the urban areas of Lille

Tropospheric ozone is a powerful oxidizing agent that may be produced by natural phenomena or the transformation of primary pollutants under the effect of sunlight. Natural conditions in the Lille agglomeration moderate the formation of tropospheric ozone (weak sunlight) and favor its dispersion through strong winds from the Atlantic. An important roadway runs through the agglomeration, used by tens of thousands of trucks per day, an important source of primary pollutants. Residential zones may have green zones as well as, sporadically, record levels of tropospheric ozone. While the primary sources are well localized, the secondary pollution formed can't be localized to the source of emissions. Ocular irritation is the most common symptom of this oxidizing agent, whose long-term effects on health are not yet well known. Ozone pollution also has an economic impact by resulting in lower agricultural yields, as ozone inhibits photosynthesis. The regulatory approach followed in France focuses on peaks in pollution, with different warning levels used. Local spikes are generally recorded depending on the vagaries of the wind in the green residential zones or vacation zones, in the absence of any primary pollutants.

A total of 100 residents of an area frequented by the "well-off" were interviewed in Marcq-en-Barœul, Lille and Villeneuve d'Ascq. Asthma is the most commonly declared pathology in the sub-sample (16%). Among the precautions that people are willing to take in the case of warnings of high levels of ozone, the least accepted are the wearing of a mask (41% intention of use), restrictions on going out (51%), and restrictions on practicing a sport in the open (53%). The most easily accepted measure was following ongoing medical treatment for respiratory problems (87%). Treatment was better accepted than prevention, with a high level of knowledge (only 5% of those interviewed declared that they had no knowledge of ozone pollution). Fifty-one percent of people knew of the link between ozone pollution and sunny weather. They also knew who was most likely to be exposed to ozone pollution, for example, 61% of those interviewed knew of the overexposure of active sports players.

The level of knowledge on ozone pollution (very well-informed, well-informed, not well-informed, or not at all informed) has an effect on the behavior of an individual. Precautions are optimally taken at the intermediate knowledge-level: there is no doubt that a very good knowledge of phenomena has a favorable influence on behavior that is safer – as well as behavior that is sometimes riskier. Today, almost no one but a volcanologist dies in a volcanic eruption. A vague threat, with no clear boundaries is undoubtedly most favorable for active attitudes of prevention. In-depth knowledge of the threat introduces finer adjustment strategies, but also induces an underestimation of the volatility of phenomena.

The residential area does not modify the perception of ozone pollution. The people interviewed did not have specific knowledge of their local environment, unlike farmers, for instance, who know where hail falls most often. They had rather fragmented information of a diffuse pollution threat; however, this situation is rather favorable to their implementation of active prevention measures.

2.5. Comparison with Morocco, the global "median" health system

Despite the progress Morocco has made in improving the quality of, and access to, health services in the recent years, social inequalities in health still persist. The mortality rate remains high, and there is still a gap between rural and urban regions. Research on risk factors for health has long followed an economic and political approach to health. Current research uses a multi-sectoral vision and interdisciplinary reflection to identify risk factors for health in the population, in order to define axes for action. For a long time, the role of material living conditions in explaining health inequalities was an established fact, and the contribution of environmental and behavioral factors to health were slower to be recognized. Today, we observe that developed and developing countries present many similarities vis-à-vis determinants for the state of health. Both types of countries are exposed to environmental risks that explain inequality in health. Despite scientific and medical progress, non-medical factors such as environmental, behavioral and lifestyle problems are recognized as risk factors. According to the WHO: "the quality of the environment and the nature of development are essential factors to health".

The environment may be a source of danger in the form of natural phenomena, economic activities (energy, industry, etc.) and human activities (habitation, workplace, etc.). Most environment-linked illnesses are caused by biological agents (bacteria, viruses, parasites, etc.), chemical agents (heavy metals, pesticides, etc.) or physical agents (harmful rays). In Morocco, the high mortality and morbidity rates may reflect insufficiencies in the health system, but are above all a reflection of environmental degradation, which is a real threat to public health. Indeed, the WHO estimates that on average, 24% of morbidity and 23% of all deaths worldwide may be attributed to environmental factors. This proportion rises to 94% for diarrheal disorders and to 41–42% for lower respiratory tract problems as well as for chronic obstructive pulmonary disease. According to the European Environmental Agency, a reduction in pollution agents and environmental stress factors could reduce death, diseases and disabilities due to the environment by 5–20%[2]. According to the WHO, environmental dangers were responsible for 18% of illnesses recorded in Morocco in 2006. Measurements of ozone levels, carbon monoxide, sulphur dioxide and nitrogen dioxide levels are higher than the prescribed norms.

The main risk factors linked to the environment are poor water quality, air pollution (atmospheric and inside residences), lack of food hygiene, inadequate sanitation, poor waste elimination, exposure to chemical products, and climatic change. Other factors, depending on the level of industrialization and urbanization in the country, are malnutrition and poverty. These factors constitute a risk for the environment and health, and must be taken seriously.

Every year, all over the world, air and water pollution and other dangers present in the environment kill over three million children below the age of five. According to the WHO, the poor quality of water causes diarrheal disorders, which are responsible for the death of 1.8 million people each year, of which 1.6 million are children younger than five years. Poor water quality is also the cause for many illnesses: cholera, dysentery, dracunculiasis, typhoid and intestinal parasites.

In the rural parts of Morocco, more than 75% of households use solid combustibles, wood, dung, coal, or agricultural waste to cook their food. These fuels give off a black smoke, which, when inhaled, causes pneumonia and other respiratory infections. Climate change and pollution have direct and indirect effects on health with heat waves, fires, storms and floods which affect harvests and freshwater reserves. The consequences of this are seen in the appearance of communicable diseases and diarrheal disorders, allergic disorders, respiratory illnesses and malnutrition.

Because of the lack of epidemiological, toxicological and biological data, which would help us establish a link between health inequalities and environmental and behavioral factors, we will examine retrospective studies on the impact of environment-related

---

2 European Environment Agency: http://local.fr.eea.eu.int/.

problems on health, and other studies that estimate that habits and behaviors are risk factors that explain the health gradient. We will examine 1) a study carried out on legionella in hot water systems in Morocco; 2) a retrospective study on death from exposure to toxic substances in Morocco; 3) a study on food and environmental factors on the risk of rhino-pharyngeal cancer; and 4) a study on pesticide poisoning carried out by the Morocco Poison Control Center.

These four studies correspond to the four areas of interest chosen in the Nord Pas-de-Calais study (today the *région* Hauts-de-France), and enable us to carry out a comparison between the two countries for a sample of themes that bring together health and environment.

2.5.1. *Risk of pesticide poisoning in Morocco*

A study carried out by the Moroccan Poison Control Center (MPCC) between January 1992 and December 2007 perfectly illustrates part of the risky behavior of people who are ignorant of the dangers that pesticides pose.

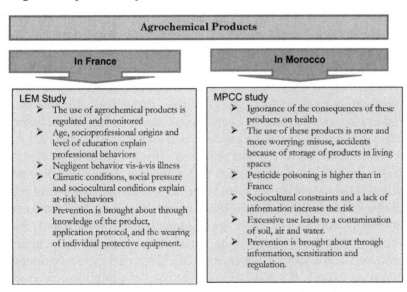

Figure 2.2. *Risks related to the handling of agrochemical products in France and Morocco*

The use of pesticides in developed countries such as France is regulated and monitored thanks to anxious and increasingly demanding public opinion. In Morocco, the use of these products is more and more worrying for several reasons: misuse of the products, the climatic conditions of the country, and ignorance of the consequences of the use of these products on the health of the farmer himself and on his environment. Morocco has one of the highest incidences of pesticide poisoning [SEM 03].

This study made it possible to demonstrate that acute pesticide poisoning represents about 11.3% of all cases of acute poisoning (2,609) that were called in to the MPCC. Agricultural products were incriminated in 38% of the cases. The majority (92%) of the poisoning cases occurred at home, and poisoning during work was 1.7%. The mortality rate was 4.8%. This number is far from reflecting reality due to the low accessibility that rural people have to the health system [RHA 09]. In this study, organophosphates were most often incriminated (28.9%). This is explained by the agricultural practices in Morocco, the ease with which these toxic products circulate and the absence of the implementation of regulations. Some professional categories (farmers) have the highest exposure and develop pathologies more easily as they frequently use large doses of the products. This can be explained through some risky behaviors that they adopt such as drinking and eating while they handle these products, which increases the risk of contamination, given that protection (gloves, masks, suits) during the use of agrochemical products is not systematic. Even though the products are delivered with user manuals, we see a gap between information on the risk and the implementation of recommendations. This is mainly explained by literacy problems and inequalities with respect to learning reading and writing. Many users do not respect the correct dosage and do not take weather conditions into consideration (wind, heat, etc.). In these cases, individuals act as per their own perception of things and take decisions that they judge to be satisfactory. Due to sociocultural constraints and a lack of information, the farmer adopts an optimistic outlook as regards the perception of the risks of using these products and commits an error of judgment by adopting risky behavior.

Even if he is the person taking the risk, the farmer is not the only person responsible for prevention. The intervention of a whole series of actors as well as the provision of proper education in good practices for handling these products is necessary. However, prevention is carried out by raising awareness among professionals, relatives and all the users of agrochemical products about the risk of poisoning.

A significant link has been demonstrated between professional exposure to pesticides and Parkinson's. In addition, the role of pesticides in the development of cancers in children has been widely studied, especially among children of farmers, who are likely to be exposed to these products in childhood. It is still difficult to confirm this due to the methodological limitations that prevent a precise evaluation of the level of exposure of these children.

The exposure to agrochemical products may also be indirect, through soil, air or water contamination. The use of these products is likely to contaminate the environment and develop pathogens. The dispersion and degradation of pesticides is triggered as soon as they are used. Infiltration and run-offs lead to the contamination of underground water tables and long-lasting water pollution. The transfer of pesticide through air is variable (25–75%) and depends on the nature of the product, weather conditions, and the frequency and mode of use.

2.5.2. Carbon monoxide poisoning in Morocco

In Morocco, CO poisoning is the main cause of death from acute poisoning. During the winter, many people use gas-heating systems and certain organic combustibles such as coal, petrol and fuel, which release carbon monoxide, a highly dangerous gas. In 2008, the National Poison Control Center declared that they had admitted 10,558 people who had been poisoned, 86% of whom were younger than 45; 66 people died.

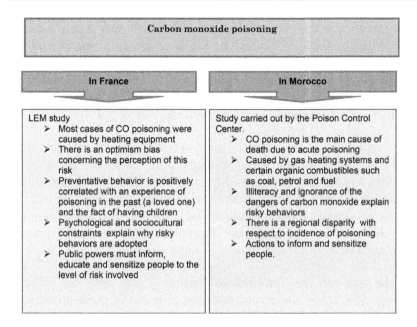

Figure 2.3. *CO poisoning in France and in Morocco*

Serious poisoning can lead to a coma followed by death. The center noted a certain regional disparity with respect to CO poisoning. The Meknès-Tafilalt region (1,603 cases and 10 deaths) and the Tétouan-Tanger region (1,529 cases and 5 deaths) registered the highest number of cases. The center declared that 90% of the poisoning cases had occurred at home. This situation can be explained by the fact that the majority of them were housewives, and most of them were poorly educated and did not know about the harmful effects of carbon monoxide.

2.5.3. *Pathologies with environment and food-related origins: rhino-pharyngeal cancer*

A study was carried out between 1996 and 2004 at the National Center for Oncology among 409 individuals who suffered from rhino-pharyngeal cancer and 394 witnesses from different regions of

Morocco (Eastern Rif in the north, Middle Atlas, and Haouz in the south). The choice of regions made it possible to show the existence of a South–North gradient for exposure to risk factors, essentially living and housing conditions, conditions in which food was stored, and hygiene. It was shown that there was a large concentration of this illness along the Fès, Tanger, Oujda axis. Among the characteristics of the population studied, it was noted that there was exposure to certain food and environmental factors that presented the risk of rhino-pharyngeal cancer in Morocco. Indeed, people frequently and regularly consumed food preserved at home, from childhood onwards until the study. Among these foods were smen[3], khlii[4], quaddid[5], spices, olives pickled in brine, and there was also the use of tagines or cocottes (utensils) to cook the food.

As concerns the characteristics of the environment, the study examined activities related to agriculture and rearing of livestock, frequent contact with toxic substances outside or within the professional context (oven smoke, smoke from *hammams*, factories, pollution from engines such as tractors, trucks, etc.), the proximity of animals, consumption of untreated water, non-daily clearing of domestic waste, illumination by candles, the absence of toilets and the practice of traditional medicine.

The results show a predominance of rhino-pharyngeal cancer among men (64.5%). Among these men, 10.5% are younger than 20 years, which means that the cancer affects the adolescent population of Morocco. In fact, the logistic regression of environmental factors has shown that life in an agricultural milieu and contact with toxic substances are significantly linked with rhino-pharyngeal cancer. These results correspond well with literature. In fact, certain illnesses such as cancers of the maxillary sinus, the larynx and of the skin are due to exposure to dust, solvents, fertilizers, pesticides, insecticides, organophosphates or phenoxyacetic acid herbicides, and UV rays [SRI 92].

---

3 Smen: butter salted and preserved, sometimes for several years, in small earthen jars.
4 Khlii: spiced meat dried in the sun and cooked.
5 Quaddid: meat that is only dried and prepared in the same manner as khlii.

The results of the study show that the absence of potable water, illumination with candles, rearing livestock, and consumption of foods such as *smen* or other pickles increase the risks of developing the illness. In addition, the East Rif region is at risk as the population practices agriculture and animal-rearing, lives in houses that are not provided with potable water, uses candles for illumination and preserves olives and lemons over long periods. In Morocco, in the rural milieu, the population uses water from wells that have not been tested and that are polluted by nitrates and nitrites, which are carcinogens. In addition, illumination using candles is a risk factor for contracting this illness. For one, the fumes released by the candles contain acrolein and acetaldehyde, which may be carcinogenic, and additionally, candles are made of glycerin, which has serious impacts on the respiratory tract. In the absence of a cooling system, people preserve foods (*quaddid, l'khlii*, olives, lemons, etc.), which allows for the appearance of mycotoxins. Analyses on samples of cereal stored in heat and in damp conditions showed the presence of Aflatoxine B1 (produced by *Aspergillus flavus*), a powerful carcinogen that plays a role in primary cancers of the liver.

The use of wood as a domestic combustible is linked to a person's milieu. This practice exposes women and children to toxic fumes, which explains the incidence of rhino-pharyngeal cancer among children in the rural milieu as well as among persons younger than 20 years living in the urban milieu and belonging to a low-income population. For the latter group, the risk of contracting the illness arises from toxic substances and exposure to pollutants such as ozone and carbon monoxide that may be absorbed during respiration through the nose. These children spend more time outdoors when the ozone levels increase, which brings us to the question of parental responsibility in educating their children and the role of public authorities in providing information and sensitizing individuals to dangers. Indeed, the better informed the parents are, the better they are at organizing the care and good conduct of their children.

Thus, Moroccan food habits are characterized on the one hand by an excessive consumption of *smen*, which is preserved in the house over years and used instead of oil in cooking tajine, couscous and harira. It has been shown that *smen* contains butyric acid known to be a powerful *in-vitro* reactivator of the Epstein-Barr virus. On the other hand, there is also the excessive use of spices such as black pepper and paprika, which constitute a health risk. Indeed, it has been reported that these spices contain amines such as piperidine and pyrrolidine, which react with sodium nitrite (used as a preservative, especially in the agro-alimentary industry, to prevent botulism) to form nitrosamines, known to induce tumors in the nasal mucus of rats and mice.

The study also showed that domestic fumes and dust released when working with marble or polishing mosaic, fumes released by Moorish baths, gas-burning machines, and by factories, etc. contain toxic substances and are risk factors for rhino-pharyngeal cancer. Finally, poisoning by plants, especially Pine thistle (*Carlina gummifera*), plays a non-negligible role in the total number of deaths. This is explained by the use of traditional medicine to cure headaches, earaches, anginas and sometimes serious illnesses such as cancer.

This study has demonstrated the importance of exposure to certain environmental factors as well as food habits, individual idiosyncrasies and lifestyles that go a great way toward explaining risky behaviors that result in illness and consequently determine health inequalities. It is also important to emphasize that this study has also revealed territorial disparities with respect to exposure to environmental risk factors.

2.5.4. Legionnaires' epidemic in Morocco

Thanks to the quality of the monitoring system, diagnostic practices and declaration, there has been widespread awareness among the public and the identification of legionella in production and distribution networks of hot water systems in Europe. In Morocco, even though this illness was introduced on the list of illnesses that must be declared since 1987, the Directorate of Epidemiology and the fight against diseases has no data on legionella. This illness is a pathology that is linked to disturbances in the environment, commonly present in water systems and transmitted to humans through the inhalation of contaminated water diffused in aerosol form. We will look at a study carried out by the Microbiology, Food Hygiene and Environment Laboratory of the Institut Pasteur in Casablanca. The study was conducted across 34 hotels and 6 residences from January to June 2008. The results of this study showed that hot water systems in Morocco were colonized by legionella bacteria (32.5% of the total number of samples analyzed). The presence of the illness was confirmed in 10 out of 34 hotels (29%). With regard to hot water systems at home, analyses showed that 50% were positive when tested for legionella. This was due to the variation in temperature in the pipe networks, which offer a large surface, creating favorable conditions for the accumulation of biofilms. The study showed that certain risk factors such as tobacco use, age, cardiomyopathy and renal pathology were linked to the lethality of legionella. This confirms that environmental factors are a determinant in exposure to a Legionnaires' epidemic. The risk can be reduced by adopting responsible behavior, implementing preventative actions and making sure all actors are well-informed: individuals, professionals and public authorities.

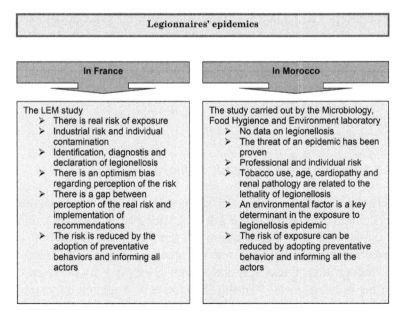

Figure 2.4. *Risk characteristics of Legionnaires' disease in France and Morocco*

The results of this study show good agreement with the study we carried out on the risk of exposure to Legionnaires' disease in the Hauts-de-France region and confirm that the environmental factors, along with the adoption of pathogenic behaviors, determine and reinforce health inequalities.

2.5.5. *Sanitation, drinking water supply and waste in Morocco*

Behavioral problems that are linked to hygiene and sanitation remain one of the principal factors of human health. In Morocco, the rural milieu as well as agglomerations such as Tanger (11 communes, about 750,000 habitants) experience difficulties with respect to sanitation and drinking water supply. In fact, sewage is poured out into a bay that covers five highly frequented beaches, due to the absence of a purification station, and this provokes diarrheal and skin illnesses.

Even in large cities such as Casablanca, we find neighborhoods that have neither electricity nor running water. Water is supplied from wells or fountains, often far away from houses. Residents store their water in cans, which provides favorable conditions for the proliferation of bacteria that cause diarrheal disorders.

Thus, uncollected waste that is neither treated nor eliminated may be a source for the contamination of drinking water and air, which causes diarrheal illnesses, respiratory disorders, gastro-intestinal disorders and skin diseases.

Air pollution (within and outside houses), difficulty of access to potable water, poor management and elimination of waste, inadequate sanitations, etc. are all risk factors for health that are linked to the environment. The existence of a strong relationship between the environment, behavior and health obliges governments and those in charge to invest in infrastructure and the skills required for managing the environment, taking health into consideration. It would be desirable to educate the community and raise awareness by improving the communication and educational systems.

2.5.6. *Atmospheric pollution and health in Morocco*

Several studies have shown the harmful effect of atmospheric pollution on health. The objective is to sensitize decision makers and the general public to a major problem that concerns both the environment and public health. We will be focusing on two of these studies:

1) The first is an epidemiological study ("Urban pollution and respiratory health: Eco-Pol study") carried out by a team of doctors from the department of Respiratory Disorders at Ibn Rochd University Hospital and the faculty of Medicine and Pharmacology in Casablanca. This study was carried out in three primary schools in contrasting zones of Casablanca and surrounding areas, namely: a central market area with high traffic density (Maârif), a zone close to industrial units and the major roadways (Roches Noires) and a peripheral zone away from any industrial activity (Dar Bouâzza). The results of the study showed that the prevalence of children presenting symptoms of asthma or allergies is considerably higher in the polluted zone (4.3%) than in the less polluted zone (1.9%). These results pushed the researchers conducting the study to call for the implementation of epidemiological monitoring systems to prevent extreme cases of atmospheric pollution and the sanitary risks that this could bring about.

2) The second study was carried out by the National Directorate of Meteorology in 2005. The results showed that the atmospheric pollution in the economic capital of Morocco is worrying. Alarm bells rang in zones such as the Zerktouni region, Sidi Othman and Ain Sbaâ. Sulfur dioxide levels are the highest in these regions, with limits exceeding the French hourly norms 484 times; the suspended particulate matter, which is presented as a dangerous pollutant, overshot the Moroccan norms 323 times, peaking at noon and in the evening. These gases can cause respiratory troubles, ocular irritations and alteration in pulmonary functions.

These studies establish a link between the increase in atmospheric pollution and the number of medical consultations, the appearance or aggravation of certain pathologies and even an increase in the mortality rates in large cities like Casablanca, which has a concentration of 40% of the industrial units in the country. The city suffers from atmospheric pollution caused by this industry and by the hundreds of thousands of cars that use poor-quality fuel, as well as heat that increases the pollution peak. According to the WHO, this chronic pollution may be the cause for early death, as well as the cause of 7–20% of cancers imputable to environmental factors. Pollution due to fuels presents a real danger to health and triggers the onset of several illnesses, notably asthma and chronic bronchitis. The consequences of such a situation place monitoring by authorities and citizens at the heart of the problem of urban atmospheric pollution. This requires surveillance campaigns and air quality control and motivating people to voluntarily carry out more frequent tests to ensure that their vehicles respect the established norms.

The figure below summarizes the levels of risk management [CAL 96] related to different hazards in France and Morocco.

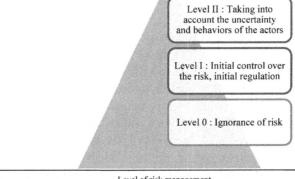

Nature of the hazard	Level of risk management	
	France	Morocco
Legionnaires' disease	Level I The Noroxo episode was a result of poor technical control over cleaning of the installation	Level 0
Carbon monoxide	Level I / level II	Level 0
Agrochemical products	Level I / Level II	Level 0
Tropospheric ozone	Level I / Level II	Level 0

Figure 2.5. *Risk management level related to different hazards in France and Morocco*

The objective of this study was to highlight the role of psychological factors in the phenomenon of health inequalities. These inequalities are presented in the form of empirical invariants, but without any wholly satisfactory explanations for this persistence. The general hypothesis for this research is, therefore, that psychological phenomena reinforce or "deepen" inequalities.

The research was carried out within a new interdisciplinary current: behavioral economics. This current ties together management, economics and psychology. It was the result of Kahneman and Tversky's criticism of the "expected utility" model used by economists. Behavioral economics borrowed two principal methodologies, Kahneman's methodology, which introduced a cognitive dimension to the analysis of rational decision-making processes, and that of Loewenstein's formation of preferences. This contribution is clearly situated within the first methodology: we hypothesize a behavior that is quite rational, a rationality that is "disturbed" but not destroyed by the cognitive reality of the decision-making processes.

One methodological point that seems to have stabilized is the definition and measurement of optimism. Following a study on behavioral finance carried out by Puri and Robinson [PUR 07], we can use three measures for optimism. We first define absolute optimism as the gap between subjective life expectancy and actuarial life expectancy. This definition is used directly in the questionnaire used for the study "Optimism and inequality". We can differentiate between conditional optimism (which depends on the knowledge of a given specific domain; for example, in response to the question: do you think you are a good driver?) and relative or social optimism (in social comparison; for example, in response to this question: do you think you are better than the average driver?). The study makes it possible to reveal the relationships between these three expressions of optimism.

The conclusions we obtain can be summarized in one proposition: the inequality gradient for health is the result of gaps that deepen based on the process of degradation or improvement of medical decisions. Poor decisions being taken with respect to one's health come from personal, familial or medical decisions or decisions by carers that have to do with prevention, the delay in turning to the health system, or the management of a treatment protocol.

The existence of a hierarchy may contribute to an improvement in decision-making processes, and it is common for the situation for employees in an organization to be better vis-à-vis a rural population. This comes back to Wilkinson's oversimplified vision, focused on the pathological effects of stress caused by the hierarchy in organizations. When it comes to health inequalities, the most critical qualities when taking medical decisions are diligence and respect for informed consent.

A brief anecdote allows us to summarize this theory of a gradient resulting from the psychological reinforcement of inequalities. A young high-school student, let us call him René, ran home on January 12, 2010 to rescue his 4-year-old little sister from under the shelter she had been in during the Port-au-Prince earthquake. René's foot was injured by a falling concrete block. A medical station was located just a short way away, but panic, caused by fear of a tsunami, resulted in René's family transporting themselves to higher ground, far away from any aid. René's state of health rapidly worsened. It was only on the seventh day after the earthquake that René was taken to a medical post where he was saved *in extremis* by urgent surgery. Handicapped, he found himself dependent on family solidarity that was not always effective.

Extreme poverty led to greater psychological "volatility". The care teams observed that there was great calm among the Haitians in the days following the earthquake. The aftermath of the catastrophe was marked by an epidemic of deep depression. The lifestyle of the poorest led to consumption modes that introduced a lot of procrastination. These lifestyles also governed and determined health issues.

How Inequalities Come Together

3.1. The interplay of the different inequalities (health, education, wealth)

Inequality has a cumulative origin that can be situated at the point of interdependence of several factors: social and geographical positions, standard of living since childhood, life events, environment, working conditions, and risky behavior. Education and income affect health in different ways. Education always has a positive impact on health, with the contribution decreasing from primary education to secondary education and with the lowest positive contribution seen in higher education. This decreasing contribution is even more marked for income – having a very high income is no longer associated with any significant gain in terms of health when compared to a high income [CUT 08]. The role of environmental factors is highly socially determined: the more developed a country, the less important the role of the environmental factors. Theories where risky behaviors are associated with social status do not completely explain the gradient: while the poor adopt more behaviors that negatively impact their health as compared to the affluent, this is not enough to explain all the differences. Over time, the dividends that education pays in terms of health increase, and this widens the gap between the most educated and the least educated in terms of health, which is not solely a result of differences in risky behavior. Addictions get fixed in adolescence, and other essential elements of one's health capital depend on familial contexts. The development of self-control is important for a whole range of pathologies. This could partly explain the benefits of education; however, access to financial resources may sometimes play a negative role by loosening the constraints that restrict access to psychotropic substances and generally resulting in poorer health practices. While existing relationships between education and health are statistically well-established, the mechanisms underlying these are still not well-explained in studies. Education contributes to temperance and self-control, and a greater respect for therapeutic protocol. It also develops personal abilities, the sense of power over one's own life and reduces depressive episodes.

A child's health is greatly impacted by their parents' incomes, and this therefore plays a role in the transfer of social status. Children who are in good health perform better at school and will have better health in adulthood. An adult's health has a large impact on their own income. One's life cycle introduces a chain of causalities that begins with health and continues to education and finally, wealth.

Figure 3.1. *The interplay of inequalities during the life cycle*

Historically, all research carried out on the causes for social inequality of health first examined the differences in living conditions, and then, from the middle of the 20th Century, approached questions linked to working conditions and access to healthcare. Inequalities result from systematic social injustice caused by a hampering of social mobility. Indeed, individuals acquire, lose or are born with capitals whether economic, cultural, social or biological (such as a chronic illness, for example). These capitals (economic, cultural, health, etc.) are built up over time, forming the basis of inequalities, unless the social system protects the mobility of professional positions.

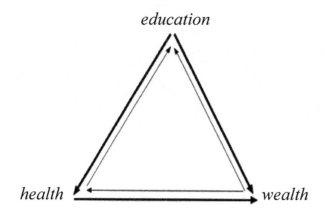

Figure 3.2. *The interdependence of inequalities*

According to the report published by Leigh *et al.* [LEI 09], poor health results in difficulties in professional integration, affects academic progress and reduces the level of education; it also has an impact on affective relationships, reducing their stability. The converse relationship is more marked in its transfer from generation to generation: the children of wealthy parents are generally in better health. Survival after five years is closely linked to the parents' affluence in a power-law relationship due to interregional global inequality.

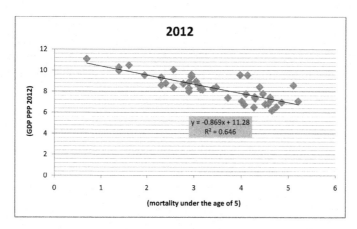

Figure 3.3. *Affluence of parents and child mortality across the world in 2012*

As stated earlier, education has a positive impact on health. For example, incomplete primary schooling is a risk factor for neurodegenerative diseases. Continued education increases one's average salary and therefore overall affluence. Large hierarchical distances in the workplace promote work-related accidents and illnesses [LEI 09].

3.2. A comparative approach

The Alma-Alta conference was marked by the driving role played by non-aligned countries, especially the African countries, which were supportive of community agents promoting health and healthcare. In the preparatory meetings for the WHO 2016–2026 program on integrated health services, all the continents were represented, and each time, about one in three countries followed a health policy that was reflected in the proposed framework. However, this alignment rate fell to 8% for the continent of Africa, being higher for Europe (55%). Thus, the criticism of a system that is overly focused on hospitals and the promotion of health is widely shared – however, countries with a higher income have today adopted the approach preached by countries of the Global South in 1978, while those countries are no longer reworking their healthcare model.

Based on the SDG criteria, countries can be divided into four groups in the 2015 ranking of health systems. The countries that promote the integrated health services framework head the list. These are mainly European countries and a few Asian countries (Singapore, Japan).

Health systems with inadequate services are found in the bottom half of the rankings. Two more intermediate groups can be identified based on the shared characteristics of their health systems.

Using this empirical approach, Iceland topped the list for 2015, based on the SDG criteria. A European survey of efficiency also ranked Iceland high on the list, although not at the top. The Icelandic health system has characteristics in common with health systems in many European countries. Iceland also has very low levels of pollution. Most of the population lives in urban zones, concentrated along the coast; there is only one university hospital, and the country has seven healthcare districts for the 320,000 inhabitants of the island. The healthcare system is universal: a residence period of six months gives you access to the social rights. The structural ratio of "doctors per bed" is 1.08, for a density of 3.2% of hospital beds. The number of intermediary health professions is double the European average, and the density of practitioners is also higher. The Icelandic health system is of the Beveridgian type; however, labor force participation is very high: only those who work on the island stay there, and the distinction between a system based on employees or residents is highly attenuated. The system is based on the rights of the patients – there is no "gatekeeper" to the health system, allowing patients to directly meet specialists without referrals. Those who wish to do so may challenge a medical decision, and the availability of pharmaceutical products is limited to 3,000 drugs. Dental care is non-reimbursable, which pegs the direct contribution of patients at exactly the same as the world average, about 18%. There is a single digitized information system for the whole island. However, some practitioners are not connected to the system, and the seven regional divisions pose practical difficulties that could have been avoided [SIG 14].

Countries with a poor healthcare offering have a low SDG score. For example, in Guinea, the "doctor per bed" indicator is 0.33, while the capacity of the health system on the whole is very low. This weakness in the Guinean system was held responsible for the recent Ebola epidemic, which highlights how the performance of the health system of the planet as a whole is so dependent on its weakest links. The Ebola epidemic of 2002 affected the African countries that followed an Alma-Alta model (such as Gabon) or an academic-humanitarian model (such as Congo), and this epidemic was contained. The catastrophic outcome of the 2013–2015 epidemic indicates that an overhaul of health systems in Africa is necessary as an epidemic threat that had, until then, been successfully contained now spread across an entire global region. The Ebola epidemic, which originated in the Guinea forest region, accounted for over 11,000 victims, 500 of whom were healthcare workers. One of the characteristics of the Alma-Alta type of health systems, already noticed in earlier epidemics, is the abnormally high mortality of health workers. Patients look for healthcare and are able to contact healthcare workers in a privileged way even before an epidemic alert is sounded.

"Alma-Alta" Health System	*"Academic-humanitarian" health system*
Universal service	Medical centers and hospitals
Public health approach	Operational capacity
Underqualified health workers	Professional ethics
Low operational capacity: for instance, only 8% of health workers in Burkina Faso have the right response to a pediatric emergency (inequality in skills).	The installed capacity covers only a part of the needs. Only areas with healthcare centers are served (spatial inequality).

Figure 3.4. *Health systems in Africa*

The explanation for why one of the sustainable development goals was not met in Burkina Faso (the goal of reducing child mortality for children younger than five years old) also incriminates an "Alma-Alta"-type health system. The Burkina Faso health system gives families good access to vaccinations and key medication. However, the healthcare workers are too poorly trained to manage the patients. Finally, only a small part of the Burkina Faso population has access to any healthcare service. Most people turn to informal care, and the poor have absolutely no access. The two dimensions of this inadequate offering (healthcare establishments and the competence of the health workers) are the basis for the inequalities in this health system [KOU 15].

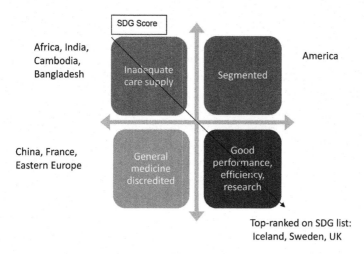

Figure 3.5. *Health systems and equity around the world*

Among the country with intermediate scores in the SDG rankings for 2015, we can distinguish two other groups, based on their health systems:

1) Latin America is characterized by high internal inequality, which is also seen in Central America and the United States. The structural ratios between the different lines of healthcare services in these health systems are equivalent to the ratios in countries ranked highest on performance. The quest for equity is seen as a new phase of development in this health system. Schematically, these health systems were all constructed like the Bismarck health systems, with social rights being reserved for paid employees. Public health concerns then led to the creation of a public organization. Certain services were developed for the poor in a selective new phase, and the result of all of this was a segmented health system, more or less universal, with very disparate service levels due to the duality inherent in the system. In this context, the promotion of integrated health services may be considered a new phase in the health system, with the objective of attaining equity [COT 15].

2) Several common characteristics are used to group a collection of other Eurasian countries in their relationship with equity, a situation of "equality through the hospital". First of all, equity here is associated

with ancient figures such as the healer Sun Simiao, a figure common to traditional and modern Chinese medicine. The structural ratios are not from the WHO model – the doctor-per-bed ratio here is about ½. The number of beds is much higher than the average in the countries that lead in the SDG rankings. Equity has, thus, been a historical concern in these countries, but is a concept that is translated today through the importance accorded to the hospital sector. Integrated health services have only been introduced on a small scale in these countries. The health organizations here have a conservative approach. Waiting time is cited by patients as the primary difficulty in access to healthcare [RAY 15]. In China, the level of care dispensed by general practitioners is better than that offered by other frontline practitioners; however, the general practitioners are stigmatized by the population [ZOU 15]. Simple measures, such as a mobile app, which facilitate the identification of referral professionals for different illnesses make it possible to improve the orientation of care and ensure continuity of care [SHI 15].

Medical densities around the world are centered on two principal modes: the first group, representing 41% of countries that share data on their medical system with international organizations, has a modal value close to that of Guinea, with one doctor for every 10,000 inhabitants. The second group of countries has a modal value of close to three doctors per 1,000 inhabitants. In the first group, integrated health services are common, but the offering of care services is inadequate. The three main countries involved in the 2013–2015 Ebola epidemics belong to this group. This group also contains South Asian countries, which are highly populated. The other large group of countries makes limited use of the integrated services policy to improve the organization of their health system.

3.3. The interplay of inequalities: from Rawls to Sen

The two most influential theoretical discussions on general health programs have been Rawl's theory of social justice and Sen's criticism of this theory. In its final form, the Rawlsian social contract is elaborated in two parts: the first is centered on a list of primary goods, and the second is the difference principle, where parliamentary political regimes establish the social minimums everyone is entitled to. Health is not a part of the first list of primary goods, as "it is a problem that must be resolved during the legislative stage, not during the original position or during the constitutional convention, as practical application in this case is partly dependent on the information available on the prevalence of different illnesses." [RAW 08, p. 235]. "These healthcare services are part of the general means required to guarantee fair equal opportunity and our ability to benefit from our basic rights and liberties and be, thus, normal and fully cooperating members of society all through our life" [RAW 08, p. 237]. Rawls had a realistic vision of international society, made up of disparate political regimes. He concluded nonetheless that we could ultimately obtain a "basic level of health services, guaranteed to everyone" [RAW 08, p. 240]. To respond to Sen's criticism, which emphasized the rigidity of the primary goods approach, Rawls brought in health as a secondary mechanism, whose share would be fixed by the parliament.

Sen's criticism introduced the actual capability that individuals have to transform primary goods into advantages for themselves: a disabled person or ill person may be unable to truly benefit from these basic rights. Rawls then emphasized that he only took into account "normal" citizens, not rationalizing situations he judged to be "extreme". Sen's approach has, since then, been divided into a large variety of "extreme" situations, such as primary dementia [LE 15]. Heckman's approach is one of those that converge with Sen's, and it introduces prioritizing the first few years of life, given the major role they play in the formation of personal capacities [NUS 12, p. 251].

The Alma-Alta declaration [WHO 78] did not strictly conform to Rawls' theoretical elaboration. It lacked the presence of public liberties in the list of primary goods. Only one broad definition of health figures in the Alma-Alta declaration. However, the declaration respects the essential elements of Rawls' approach: in a tradition that goes back to Rousseau, knowledge-dimension and skill are absent. Inequality of health is presented here as a moral scandal, and realism leads to the delivery of a minimum level of primary care. The Alma-Alta declaration is situated in an intergovernmental framework and one of international realism. This strives to maximize a minimum, bringing about a difference through the local means allocated to the health sector by the domestic authorities.

For the large organizations that work with children and in medical care around the world, the specific funds that they have already developed form the alternative and complementary model to the Alma-Alta declaration. Disaster medicine goes against Rawls' rules on setting aside extreme cases and focusing on the situation of the poorest; instead, here people must consider extremes while applying the common professional care practices. The unique nature of humanitarian medicine lies in its standardization of processes: equipment kits, the use of pre-established, limiting lists. The risks of war impose limits on movement and require good coordination and appropriate stock management [BRA 04].

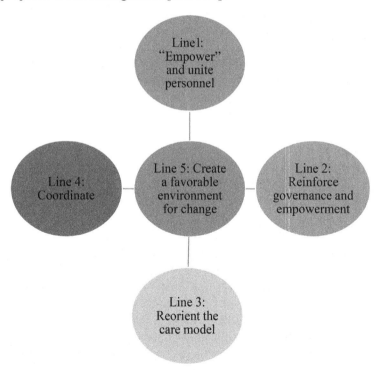

Figure 3.6. *The axes of the WHO's integrated health services program*

Point 1.4 of the WHO framework [WHO 15] on integrated health services introduces the concept of equity by explaining that it is essential to implement universal cover, one of the goals in the SDG. The aim is to reach out to populations that are poorly served or marginalized. The first point is devoted to "empowering people" or making them independent. This therefore takes into account Sen's critique on the effectiveness of rights to health. This change, however, is only partial. The health objectives in the SDG are modest, and the indicators necessary for the implementation of integrated health services are not yet fixed and may never be. The general WHO context of intergovernmental governance and the reaffirmation of continuity with the primary care policy of the Alma-Alta declaration are limiting factors in the general introduction to the principle of equity that is discussed in point 1.4.

Convergence toward a universal health system with a minimum level of care remains in line with the functional principle of large intergovernmental organizations. However, this approach has been plunged into difficulty with tragic issues such as the Ebola fever, which developed in the Guinea forest region, as this "Rawlsian" strategy does not make it possible to guarantee minimum security across the health system.

PART 2

Sustainable and Equitable Architecture for Health Systems

Transformations in Health Systems

4.1. Sustainability of health systems

André Grimaldi [GRI 16] proposes the following definition for integrated healthcare, at the heart of a general redefinition of sustainable structures for health systems:

> "The best-suited model is that of "integrated medicine", which is simultaneously biomedical, pedagogic, psychological as well as social. It is medicine that is personalized across all these four elements, a partnership-based medicine that assumes a rapport, asymmetrical undoubtedly, but an egalitarian one, with the patient. Thanks to the therapeutic education of the patient and the empathy shown by the caregiver, each can partly take the place of the other while retaining their own role. Finally, it is a medical system that is coordinated between the township and the different health establishments and between the various professionals (doctors, paramedic workers and social workers) developing consistent practices and working in a complementary manner to achieve shared objectives and delivering concordant messages to patients and their entourage" [GRI 16].

Questions about sustainability arose due to the changes in pathologies and the lengthening of lifespans, changes in the forms of financing, incentive structures and specific organizational structures to ensure that there was continuity in care. "Integrated healthcare" also includes telemedicine, management of an individual's health data and social support through social networks.

Since the 19th Century, the health system has been built around the management of patients in acute phases. Foucault explains why the emergence of the clinic under the French Revolution took so long [FOU 63]: the revolutionaries' pursuit of complete decentralization, in other words, down to the isolated individual, had a paralyzing effect on any reorganization of medicine. The debate over the WHO Alma-Alta charter returned to a similar opposition in views: on the one hand, there was the strictly political idea of the social contract, where medical knowledge is without power and does not exist in the organizational schema, and on the other hand, academic and humanitarian standards oriented toward the skills of a qualified staff.

The SDG objective of universal cover for the period between 2015 and 2030 does not seem unrealistic. There is however the fear that this universal service will materialize in the form of a very casual telemedicine system. If medical equipment is spatially distributed in a distribution whose major mode is about two beds per thousand, the distribution of the practitioners is bimodal, with some countries marked by the near absence of physicians – 41% of countries declaring their health statistics to the WHO – and other countries with values just around 3%. There is, therefore, no technological split but a large-scale as well as a small-scale problem with spatial inequality around the world. Medical deserts, or regions or communities without doctors, contrast areas that are well-equipped and served by trained medical staff.

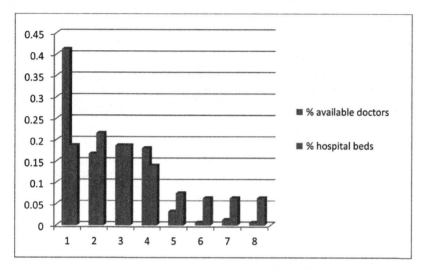

Figure 4.1. *Countries lacking in doctors and beds (<0.1%) to countries with many beds (>0.4%)*

According to Olivier de Sardan's analysis [OLI 15], sustainability in health systems in the Sahel zone is based on the existence of smugglers between the two parts of the system: the petty bureaucracy of the public health system and the local NGOs integrated into international networks. These NGOs are financed per fixed-term-project, and therefore the successes they achieve must be capitalized by internal leadership within the local petty bureaucracy. Sustainability depends on the organizational provisions for change management in both the parts of the health system, the petty bureaucracy as well as the enterprising NGOs. Long training periods for healthcare workers are another important parameter in the sustainability of health systems as well as the management of a regular supply of medication. In the countries studied, these are generally best organized by the NGO sector, which fulfill the single mission of providing access to the most disadvantaged populations [OLI 15].

March's [MAR 91] theoretical contribution to the exploration/ exploitation dilemma can be read in terms of sustainability. This contribution offers an explanation for the limited lifespan of for-profit organizations: the learning curve is shorter for the exploiter than for the explorer – so much so that commercial structures disappear due to the internal absence of the explorer and the necessary renewal in a changing environment. Structures that are strongly linked to the explorer have very long lifespans, but a more unstable financial equilibrium. In addition, they generate spatial inequalities: Raynaud [RAY 15] shows that inequalities in the field of health remain dependent on the location of universities, as graduates prefer the neighborhood in which they have studied when choosing where to practice professionally. Similarly, the initial diffusion of major therapeutic innovations is often limited to their region of origin; for instance, the bistoury, which comes from the name of a small Italian town Pistoia, which has a hospital founded in 1270. Designing sustainable and equitable structures makes it possible to bring together the exploiter for equity and the explorer for sustainability. The organizations that make up the health systems bring together institutional longevity and spatial inequality of "medical deserts", that is, they present the characteristics of an exploiter/explorer balance that is favorable to the explorer, which is in contrast to the results common to purely commercial organizations.

4.1.1. *Sustainability and life cycle*

Angus Deaton [DEA 13] presented a global epidemiological transition: longer lifespans, a reduction in infectious disease mortality, and an increase in long-term care. Infectious disease mortality reduced significantly, which brought about a large gain in life expectancy in emerging and developing countries.

To illustrate this transition, let us analyze the case of dementia. The prevalence of dementia is approximately 50 million people worldwide, most of whom are in emerging or developing countries. The evolution of health systems may be schematized based on the existing tripartite decomposition of health systems.

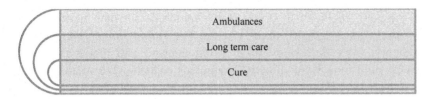

Figure 4.2. *Simplified flowchart of a health system*

4.1.2. *Cures*

This involves those parts of the health system that make up its matrix. Cure is one dimension that has existed since the origin of medicine. Taking just dementia as an example, the various types of dementia were approached differently in the earliest medical systems. Ancient Greek medicine, for example, separated the "divine" forms from the forms that were scientifically studied, such as epilepsy, without explicitly mentioning primary dementia. Delusions and intoxication had a positive status (the intoxication of Noah in the Old Testament); in China, the mythical hero Yu the Great was paralyzed on one side.

Dementia was more directly approached by ancient Chinese and Indian medicine. In the classical treatise on internal medicine, *The Yellow Emperor*, the oldest preserved collection on acupuncture; it is said a patient with dementia must not be turned away. The doctor must go to their house to adjust prescriptions. It was, in essence, a statement of the principle of individualizing treatment for dementia.

Hua Tuo (140–208) also spoke of dementia, which he attributed to a lack of energy. One description focused on an 80-year-old man with a fragile spirit and incoherent expression. The man had low *qi*, the vital energy, in his lungs. Zhang Zhongjing (150–219) indicated that dementia had a vascular origin. For Sun Simiao (581–682), individuals over 50 years of age had deficiencies in memory due to low *qi* in their kidneys. Sun Simiao described the natural history of the illness and gave the first description of a degenerative disorder and progressive dementia. Hong Mai (1123–1202) described "a person who cannot recognize anyone", situating himself within the original theory of the visceral origins of dementia.

Ancient medical theories were centered on the humors and disorders that originated in the viscera. The *Yellow Emperor* explained dementia by a deficiency of *qi* (vital energy) and blood stasis (to which delusions were directly attributed), which were treated using potions [LIU 12].

The therapeutic remedies used in traditional Chinese medicine [ZEN 15, LIN 15] offer alternatives to medication that is contraindicated for neurodegenerative disorders (such as the class of benzodiazepines to treat long-term sleep disorders and anxiety). Available medication has a very low effect. Approaches that use exercise have a greater effect on cognitive indicators [STR 15]. The costs measured in China were mainly informal and related to the loss of functions [KU 16]. The recommendations in Asia are to increase the social sector and deploy strategies to maintain the functioning of people with disorders; these recommendations reflect situations that are common to all the countries in the world [KU 16].

4.1.3. *Long-term care*

The hospital as we know it today was introduced quite late. Medical explanations using humors and viscera were first challenged. In China, dementia was localized to the cerebral region toward the end of the 18th Century. Wang Qingren (1768–1831) observed atrophy in the brains of patients suffering from dementia. In Europe during the Enlightenment, the Swiss physician Bilguer recommended that those who were wounded in war be treated in hospitals. Eighteenth-Century medicine was based on the early recommendations of hygiene in hospitals and the first drugs and antiseptic medication against pain, malaria and fevers. Medicine in Ancient Greece had emerged around the treatment of malarial patients. The clinic became a generalized concept in the 19th Century [FOU 63], a time when most widespread pathologies were infectious diseases (diarrheal disorders, tuberculosis, childhood infectious diseases). Not only is the hospital as an institution relatively recent, but it has quite some difficulty in distinguishing long-term care from planned treatments.

4.1.4. *Ambulances*

The concept of mobile care units providing immediate help to patients emerged toward the end of the 18th Century (the first horse-drawn ambulances in France date back to Napoleon Bonaparte's armies), especially taking into account the risk of hospital-acquired infections inherent to the institution of the hospital. The best armies introduced ambulance services during the Napoleonic wars. These services became widespread only from the end of the 19th Century in Europe. They were introduced in China by the grandson of one of the founders of the Red Cross, the Canadian practitioner Norman Bethune.

The epidemiological transition took place in the second half of the 20th Century. Schematically, before this transition, health systems remained within the framework where treatment was conceived of as a series of operational steps. After the transition, healthcare was organized into three different concepts of time: a time of programmed treatment (the cure), a time requiring emergency response (ambulances), and the long-term care time of other problems, such as primary dementia.

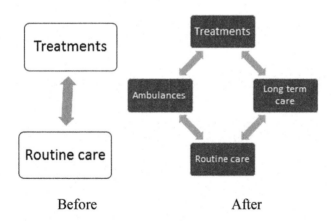

Before   After

Figure 4.3. *Long-term evolution of health systems*

The diagnostic rate for dementia varies across the world, between 3% in Hungary and 55% in Sweden; it is 7% in China [CHE 13]. Access to care, domestic relations and attitudes to general medicine contribute jointly to the number of patients diagnosed. The contribution of each of these factors differs for different regions around the world. Domestic settings play a negative role in two configurations: one where the patient is isolated, and also in a joint family structure (domestic paternalism). The density of general practitioners (GPs) is often determined by healthcare administrations, such that the same number of GPs for 100,000 inhabitants can correspond to varied rates of diagnosis. The care rate for dementia is equal to that for mental health [CHE 13]. For instance, the cohort study carried out in Auvergne on the stigma attached to dementia resulting from neurodegenerative disorders brought health practitioners to the fore rather than families. Professional ethics combined with an intra-family decision-making system is brought to the fore in China [FAN 04, FAN 11].

Well-organized mental health and social work fields are the precursors to well-organized care for dementias. The coordination between the different fields (health, mental health, social) remains a major difficulty, affecting the deployment of care for dementia. Sweden is cited as a positive example for its organizational schema that combines the different parts of the health system [ROS 11].

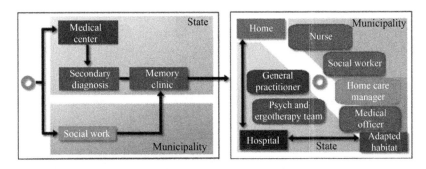

Figure 4.4. *The Swedish health system and the care for dementia*

Transforming the healthcare offering is an organizational change, which begins with healthcare systems that have been able to structure themselves around recurrent difficulties. Malaria played a major role in the structuring of medicine in the Ancient Greco-Roman world, just as treating infectious, environment-related illnesses promoted the institutionalization of hospital in the 19th Century. This was despite the risk of hospital-acquired illnesses having been clearly described by John Pringle in the 18th Century. The situation in Ancient China was different, with the local flora there providing the best-known anti-malarial treatment. The ethical recommendations for the individualization of care for dementia have a long history here, dating back to the first written medical texts.

The historical dynamic in health systems between *Risk* and *Care* seems more dependent on the second term than on the first. *Artemesia annua* is a Chinese plant that provides the most effective treatment yet for malaria. The knowledge of this simple treatment in ancient Chinese medicine meant that malaria had seemingly no major role to play in structuring the ancient Chinese system of medicine, whereas the growth of malaria in the Mediterranean zone resulted in medical institutions being strongly structured around providing care to malarial patients by the doctors in Ancient Greece. "Difficult problems" can have a large structuring effect on health systems. Dementia was already a "difficult problem" for doctors in ancient China.

4.2. New professions – new ethics?

The transformation of a health system results in new fields being created. Does this lead to changes in professional ethics? Among the new fields and positions created, we have the "case manager", who takes charge of the arrangements and readjustments required for patients for whom the follow-up happens at home. In Germany, case managers are mostly trained in nursing care and are appointed for a year; in other countries where this position exists, care managers are entrusted with about 40 cases. These managers have acquired the skills required for medical or social care. Econometric studies show a correlation between the growing care for dementias and the density of social work, and the field of mental health.

4.2.1. *Case managers*

A case manager is a professional with a specific deontology. Their main tasks are to protect the interests of the patient, protect their autonomy and support their caregivers. Existing charters of professional ethics for care managers reproduce the broad principles of medical ethics. For example: the English Case Manager Code outlines "minimal ethics" (the content of this will be discussed in the next section), to which is added professional integrity, an exhortation to speak the truth and to promote the legal rights of the patient. Professional ethics combine the *Risk* aspects related to the existence of vulnerabilities resulting from neurodegenerative diseases and the *Care* dimension that covers both the natural caregivers and the patient. The common thread between these professional ethics is the question of truth. Maintaining the functioning of the patient, that is, protecting their autonomy, results from a combination of taking into account the patient's preferences and social costs, and this is true even when the benchmark social ethics are community based [KU 16].

Takeo Doi [DOI 88] carried out an analysis of Japanese society, as a society marked by affective dependence, and which places a premium on feminine attention toward others (*amae*). The ethics of *amae* are in contradiction to the ethics of independence. *Amae* places a premium on the need for dependence fostered by the group or by an organization. The ethics of caring for others, as described in the Japanese society, is conducive to the deployment of care managers and for caring for dependent senior citizens. This tolerant and sociable society also has its flaws, as diagnosed by Takeo Doi [DOI 88]. The ethics of *amae* are rather in conflict with the ethics of governance. The conduct of organizations within the framework of these ethics is based on group solidarity, which is conducive to covering up wrongdoing, complicity between inspection bodies and operating companies. The term *amakudaru*, used for those who carry out the ethics of *amae*, finds itself translated into articles of the penal codes in other countries! These have to do with revolving door practices – making use of a public function to procure the advantage of a position in the private sector. The positive status given to indulgence in Japanese society aggravates the problems in coordination. The patient care system is complex, and in a comparative study of Alzheimer plans, the best examples are those taken from the UK or Sweden. The ethics of *amae* were incriminated in the crisis in the Japanese society, pushed to the wall after the tsunami of 2011, with a general reform of the oversight of organizations and institutions that were forced to abandon cronyism and revolving door practices.

4.2.2. The general practitioner's concern for others

GPs in France are trained to be gently directive. For instance, casually slipping an anodyne, "Have you already considered quitting smoking?" into the conversation. However, attitudes beyond these official "parental" norms have been observed in controlled studies [BLO 15]. Balint's theory outlined the "Apostolic" ethics that he observed among GPs, who had a tendency to idealize a receptive and cooperative patient. GPs felt that they did not always have the appropriate means at their disposal to smoothly manage the care of patients who are judged "unteachable" [BLO 15].

GPs and hospital staff often bring to the fore their capacity for empathy. Case managers insist on the ethics of truth telling. This is enshrined in their ethical code. Regulations require that patients be informed. For example, in China, the GP is supposed to provide all the information to the patient or to a family member. However, medical and domestic paternalism come together and contribute to the low rates of care for those with dementia.

Chen Yugi's domestic paternalism (–215, –150) dates back to Ancient China: the medical diagnosis is given to a family member, but not directly to the patient. The family remains the authority that will take charge of the person with dementia. In the Confucian tradition, independence is only at the family level.

Medical paternalism is defined as the withholding of a diagnosis by the healthcare worker. This happens quite often for dementias: there was a 95% withholding rate for Alzheimer's disease (AD) as late as 2000 in England. When it comes to cancers, the attitude of the GPs in Europe has shifted from an attitude of withholding toward an ethical practice of telling the truth. Chinese studies on GPs reveal professionals who are concerned about the equitable treatment of patients. In regions where Buddhism has a strong influence, this compassionate attitude is even stronger. Professional burn-out tends to particularly affect these professionals [TSA 14].

In summary, the professional ethics involved in caring for those with dementia combine recommendations both from the *care* and *risk management* dimensions. Neither empathy nor risk management can claim to be all-sufficient for defining these professional ethics [COR 13]. While there is a dividing line, this is mainly between the different forms of paternalism and an ethics of truth telling. The existence of this line is reflected in the care rate for dementias.

4.2.3. *"Minimal" professional ethics*

The problem before us is that of the development of a care structure that makes it possible to provide care to patients with neurodegenerative disorders. As the communication abilities of these patients progressively deteriorate, they are particularly vulnerable and have reduced access to different forms of political expression. High-quality procedures require, on the one hand, a risk analysis, while on the other hand, the most common forms of dementia lead to patients being hypersensitive about any breach of solicitude and care [CAR 15]. The development of structured care services is, therefore, dependent on an addition of recommendations, benevolent procedures having been added to quality and risk management (to turn to the terms used in France).

❶ The genesis of professional ethics in the field of health accompanies improvements in teaching methods. The earliest bioethical treatises of the Tang dynasty in China appeared during the time that written exams became common. In these ethical recommendations, it was stipulated that students must be very diligent in their studies in order to avoid diagnostic errors. It was earlier prescribed that the student be obedient to his teacher, which led to difficulties in maintaining quality of care. Confucius proposed that there be the ethics of respect for authority and of compassion. Under the Tang dynasty, the emperor officially recognized that medical diagnostics are independent of the official truth of divination methods.

❷ One of the criticisms leveled at the ethics of autonomy comes from the ethics of care, which explores ethics formulated around compassion and community [TRO 12]. These approaches have been developed since the ancient world, until a shift was introduced by the ethics of truth, the first evocations of which came from the Cynical philosophers of the ancient Greco-Roman world.

❸ Critiquing medical competence is an intellectual tradition that dates back to Rousseau. While the Alma-Alta declaration comes from this current of thought, the case is different for humanitarian medicine: "free access for all to effective healthcare, that is, provided by trained personnel, with appropriate means, this is the only equitable policy" [BRA 09].

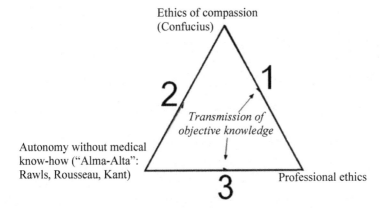

Figure 4.5. *The transformation of ethics*

It is difficult to decide on the optimal care structure in the case of AD and related dementias. If a treatment that provided significant benefits to the patient were to be developed, it would considerably modify public health policy for dementias (Barnett *et al.*, 2014). Willingness to pay for diagnosis covers exams such as psychometric tests. The amount agreed upon is insufficient for complete exploration using medical imagery [MÜH 16]. This significant willingness to pay indicates, however, the validity of prioritizing sharing the truth with the patient. Once a diagnosis is presented, there exists the risk of over-medication. For example, abusively diagnosing a person with cognitive difficulties as presenting a pre-dementia situation and prescribing medication that has no effect [STR 15]. There may be poor coordination between care services [NAK 14] or gaps in care provided. The estimations based on a large-scale survey are quantitatively the highest for this last group [CHE 13].

Several typologies have been proposed to organize all the systems of ethics used in the world. Ogien [OGI 07] suggested differentiating between "minimal" and "maximal" bioethics. To complement this, Schweder [SCH 00] developed a universal typology with respect to the ethical situation in Asia and around the world. Schweder suggested differentiating between ethics prioritizing autonomy, ethics prioritizing the community (Schweder emphasized that the Chinese context was the example for this kind of ethics) and ethics of purity (following a logic completely in contrast to the ethics of risk management). In ethics that prioritize the community, the moral code gives special weight to duties, respect and obedience toward authority; actions must be in accordance with what is expected from one's role, gender and age. In ethics that prioritize "purity", the individual must remain pure and just, avoiding pollution or corruption. Moral codes of purity focus on bodily habits and sexual and dietary taboos. The definition of an ethical system for the care of patients with AD is more delicate in the context of this moral code. The expressions of these different ethical systems in the domain of health may be minimal or maximal. Ruwen Ogien characterizes the ethics of autonomy, as laid out by Kant, as being maximal, as it includes dispositions toward oneself, positive duties toward others and toward collective entities (society, the army, etc.).

4.2.4. *Three conditions for a minimal system of ethics*

Ruwen Ogien [OGI 07] proposed three conditions for ethics in general and especially for ethics in the context of health:

1) Benevolence, defined as non-sacrifice in the sense of not harming another. More detailed explanations for benevolence were put forth by Confucius. This is a virtue that must be developed from a sense of humanity. This recommendation was reformulated by Mencius in an expression equivalent to *"primum non nocere"*, which was also chosen by Ogien [OGI 07]. For Mencius, benevolence means, above all, not causing harm. In ethical codes on providing care to patients with AD, this benevolence is explained as a double injunction against "abandonment of care" as well as "unreasonable obstinacy" (Alzheimer's Charter, 2011).

2) Non-discrimination is the second principle proposed by Ruwen Ogien [OGI 07]. Chinese practitioners cite this as their first principle given the charter for medical deontology formulated forth by Sun Simiao (581–682), which announces a universal principle for access to healthcare. He also gave the first description of the progression of dementia. Care must be individualized: in the *Yellow Emperor*, the treatise on internal medicine, dementia leads to a medical decision and is different from the general precepts and routine prescriptions for other pathologies. In contemporary charters, "any patient with illness must be able to benefit from progress made in research" (Alzheimer Charter, 2011).

3) Neutrality is the respect for another's life choices, and this is the third of the principles listed by Ruwen Ogien [OGI 07]. This neutrality is detailed in contemporary ethical charters (for example, the first five points of the ten on the Alzheimer Charter of 2011 have to do with neutrality: "recognize the right of the patient to be, to feel, to desire and to refuse; respect the choice of the patient; respect the patient, protect their goods and their material choices; respect the affective relations of the patient; respect the citizenship of the patient").

In practice, with respect to these three conditions, different forms of paternalism (a lack of respect for neutrality) are indicated as one of the explanations for the low care rates for patients throughout the world (three out of four do not receive care according to the WHO). Community ethics, like the Confucian ethics, fulfill the first two conditions, but are less satisfactory as concerns the third condition. It is necessary for *Care* distribution to be weighted and measured, as indicated in the Alzheimer's Charter of 2011, for instance. This weighted distribution has also figured in the oldest known medical text. The absence of solicitude is a risk; so is the exhaustion of caregivers who are overwhelmed by their duty. Prescribing moderation in caregiving is necessary in ethics for healthcare workers.

It is possible, undoubtedly, to compare *Care* ethics with the tradition of community-based ethics using, for example, Confucius' first injunctions. Ruwen Ogien (2012) highlights two pitfalls in the development of an ethics for *Care*: paternalism (due to the absence of explicit injunctions for neutrality) and inequality (due to the absence of indications on weighting *Care*).

People with frontotemporal dementia (FTD) have a decline in empathy and "care-based" morality. All dementias are associated with an increase in "rule-based" morality, and patients are more sensitive to infractions of routines, rules and conventions. In addition, patients with AD are more receptive to infractions of "care-based" morality.

%	FTD	AD	Control group
Care-based	15.8	21.77	19.2
Rule-based	13	10.45	9

Figure 4.6. *Comparative moralism based on dementias (source: [CAR 15])*

The original matrix for *Care* ethics was Gilligan's criticism of Kohlberg's development psychology. Neurodegenerative illnesses are characterized by functional decline, the converse of the cognitive and moral development during adolescence in the initial debate between psychometry and *Care* ethics.

Dementias are located between *Risk* and *Care*. Black and white strategies, which focus entirely on *Risk* or entirely on *Care* are invalidated. Joan Tronto [TRO 12], proposed that a dividing line between *Risk* and *Care* must be specified for the case of neurodegenerative illnesses. There are indeed domestic and medical paternalisms on the one hand, and on the other hand, the ethics of truth. The situation here is comparable to that of cancers, but with an ethics for truth that seem much weaker in the case of AD and related illnesses.

In Ulrich Beck's sociology of risk, medicine is an example of a sub-political system whose decisional circuits are largely out of the purview of parliamentary control [CAL 15]. It is possible to identify different sources of social losses: paternalisms, poor coordination between care services, and forms of over-medicalization that are observed in treatment protocols (for example, the systematic screening for neurodegenerative diseases). *Care* ethics are seen as a willingness to battle paternalisms – Beck's sociology of risk raises concerns about all the forms of technocracy, even medical technocracy. Syncretism between these two approaches would be desirable for the healthcare services that control the sources for different social losses – not technocracy, nor paternalism.

4.3. Decentralization and equity

Decentralization is necessary. While the optimal health policy is context-dependent, this is also often true for the optimal size of a healthcare zone. Assuming the existence of a two-level system and restricting ourselves to this, as in the example of the Finnish health system cited below, certain health problems often extend across large regions. Examples of this include air pollution and disasters. Other problems are better treated by a narrower approach. The procedure implemented is sometimes experimental: the Icelandic health system is today considered the finest in the world, but its information system has large scope for improvement due to hesitations over what must be assigned to a local level and what must be made accessible across the entirety of the network.

Decentralization in terms of training leads to "stowaway" behavior: regionalization of training in Germany led to an underinvestment in training, with each region counting on its neighbors to provide the necessary skills. In addition, graduates often tend to settle close to their place of training, and a combination of these strategies would explain the global paucity of qualified healthcare personnel. Voluntary migration politics, such as the Japanese nursing program in the Philippines, for example, have not met with the expected success, as linguistic and cultural training had to be added to the acquisition of professional competencies.

Finland is one of the promoters of the WHO's integrated health services program. The Finnish system, adopted in 2010, integrates a network of large hospitals into a broad-access information network – the KEKSI information system. The narrower system contains the frontline and secondary line healthcare services, such as the EKSOTE system for example in the Lappeenranta (72,000 inhabitants, a hospital and two universities for a total of 12,000 students). Three other agglomerations complete this regional schema for South Karelia.

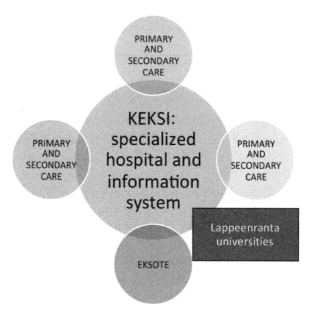

Figure 4.7. *Integrated health services in South Karelia (Finland)*

One of the limitations of decentralization is the existence of risks that can only be managed on a large scale, such as catastrophes or atmospheric pollution. A study of existing documentation indicates that programs to reinforce resilience to catastrophes do exist. This consolidation must be carried out before the appearance of any catastrophe – that is, there must be an "upstream" integration of services. The gaps between literature and practices in the field have mostly to do with risks whose prevention policies must be broken down on a smaller scale.

The French law of January 2016 proposes the experimental setting-up of a local team to prevent loss of autonomy for senior citizens above the age of 75 years. This is a positive example of "upstream" integrated health services – services that are not confined only to outpatient support ("downstream" integrated care).

Risk	Natural zone	Upstream integrated care	Global median	Example: France
Disasters	Large area	2	0	1.5
Air pollution	Large area	2	0	1.5
Legionnaire's disease	Commune	1.5	0	1
Carbon monoxide	Commune	1.5	0	1.5
Pesticides	Commune	1.5	0	1.5

Figure 4.8. *Decentralization and risks (LEM study, 2008)*

Integrated health services are commonly practiced in medical NGOs, the positive actors in the Ebola tragedy in West Africa. The weaknesses in the health systems in the three countries struck by the Ebola epidemic of 2014–2015 as well as the WHO's denial of an epidemic risk considerably weakened the credibility of intergovernmental organization and national approaches. The definition used by the WHO to define integrated care is unclear, always providing small loopholes for health systems that are notoriously underestimated, which were involved in the burgeoning Ebola episode. In 2017, the G-20 will decide on the global health policy. The magnitude of the paradigm shift provoked by the Ebola crisis will then be re-evaluated, especially the role of the WHO which previously focused only on the regulation of health and which was taken by surprise by the Ebola epidemic.

The WHO working group study on integrated health services is incomplete. There is no definition of the indicators to monitor the level of integration of health systems. The different issues of inequality in health demand answers in the form of highly specialized actions which, on the whole, remain completely undefined.

5

Integrating Innovation

The main objective of any health system is to improve health. One of the key elements in achieving this is to integrate technological progress in the field and innovations into the system. While these advancements mainly concern the production sector, other sectors in the health system are also involved, including the integration of new technology in the pharmaceutical industry, the digitization of the healthcare system, remote management of a medical protocol, a diagnosis or medical equipment, health services at home and new coordination within the health system.

Within the framework of these new health systems, among the topics relating to the success of innovations, there are two important approaches to consider. The first is the exploitation/exploration model in healthcare organizations. This is followed by the relationship between social and economic utility. We will, therefore, first study innovations through the prism of the exploitation/exploration model. We will then examine how the endogenous growth theory has contributed to understanding the link between incentives and innovation, and Corporate Social Responsibility, which will open up new possibilities and ideas on the link between innovation and social utility.

However, before beginning any analysis of innovations in health systems, we must first define innovation, the types of innovation, its current characteristics and existing healthcare fields.

5.1. Defining innovation

It was through technology that the concept of innovation first entered the discourse on research. This is why we often think of innovation as technological progress, forgetting that it may also be a social phenomenon. For example: money, laws, marriage, the modern State, Taylorism, education or health systems – all these are just a few examples of key social innovations in the evolution of modern societies [DAN 05].

Among the foremost definitions of innovation, as used in the scientific world, is the definition proposed by the Oslo manual [OEC 05], according to which, "technological innovations cover technologically new products and processes as well as significant improvements in existing products and procedures". "Innovation goes beyond research and development. Far from being limited to research laboratories, the field of innovation encompasses the full range of users, suppliers and consumers – whether this be in public administration, enterprises or in not-for-profit organizations – and this transcends national, sectorial or institutional borders" [OEC 05].

5.1.1. *The types of innovation*

Based on the third edition of the Oslo manual [OEC 05], we can distinguish four types of innovation:

– Product innovation: the introduction of a new good or service. This definition includes marked improvement to technical specifications, components and materials, of integrated software, user-friendliness or other functional characteristics.

– Process innovation: the implementation of a new or markedly improved production or distribution method. This concept involves significant changes in techniques, material and/or software.

– Innovation in marketing: the implementation of a new marketing method involving significant changes in the design or conditioning, placement, promotion or pricing of a product.

– Organizational innovation: the implementation of a new organizational method for organization practices, the organization of a workspace or in the company's external relationships.

All four types of innovation can be seen in health systems:

– Product innovation: new drugs, robotics, bionic prosthetics, 3D imaging, etc.

– Process innovation: DNA sequencing and targeted medicine, gene therapies, biotechnology, targeted therapy, etc.

– Marketing innovation: telemedicine, sale of medication over the Internet, E-health, etc.

– Organizational innovation: innovation in the modes of providing care, introduction of E-health within the organization, new professional practice methods, shared medical files, platforms for remotely follow-up, therapeutic education, connected patients, coordination in the care journey.

These innovations occur within the context of globalization. They are characterized by the fact that they are no longer rare, but instead very frequent, they are generalized and open; they are also situated in an economic system based on continuous innovation.

In fact, across scientific literature, there is agreement on the utility of innovation in improving health. Innovations in the field of health must keep pace with evolutions in the technological, engineering and social sectors in order to achieve the objectives of human well-being and confronting health inequalities. Examining the exploration/ exploitation approach will allow us to better understand the utility of continuous innovation.

5.2. Using the exploration/exploitation model

March [MAR 91] used an economic approach that deals with the question of innovation in perpetual evolution. In his definition of two-state, March contrasts exploration and exploitation. Exploration is searching for and experimenting with new ideas and alternatives, which are often uncertain, while exploitation refers to the use, refinement and extension of pre-existing technologies and competencies.

Exploitation has predictable, near-certain short-term gains, and the organization of an exploitation activity does not require an additional adaptation effort as it is has already been tried and stabilized. Exploration, on the contrary, necessarily goes through adaptation and experimentation before the results can be stably used. This is why organizations prefer exploitation to exploration.

The risk of innovating within the exploitation framework (introducing only minor improvements, in technology, for instance) is that you can find yourself completely left behind by new innovations (new technologies or processes) which are often better performing. This reduces the ability to adapt to changes in the market, which is also evolving more and more rapidly. The life cycle of products and technologies has become so short that an organization must be run with an optimal combination of exploitation and exploration.

In March's model, the process of exploitation makes it possible to use the return on investments to, first of all, finance early phases of exploration. Second, it makes it possible to continue to evolve through cumulative learning. As concerns the process of exploration, it makes it possible to react appropriately to sometimes radical changes in the organization's environment (competition, market, etc.).

As concerns innovation, the problem that each sector of activity faces at the macro-economic level is the lack of consistent administration that would enable them to optimize the combination of exploration and exploitation processes. This is all the more true in the case of the healthcare sector or health industry. In addition to the lack of governance, the health sector also suffers from a lack of capital to finance development costs (the cost that separates an invention from its introduction on the market).

Consistent governance of the health system makes it possible to integrate all the key actors of innovation into its economic model, while optimizing the exploration/exploitation combination and taking into consideration the environmental assets unique to each health system.

In France, for example, the European Commission has identified four main assets for competitiveness that result from the capacity for innovation inherent to the French health system:

1) Highly developed biomedical research: France is ranked among the top five countries around the world in scientific production in the fields of life sciences and health. On average, 21,500 biomedical research articles are published every year, 5% of which are considered to be articles of excellence.

2) A very solvent and large domestic market: one of the advantages of the health system model in France is that it promises innovations a definite solvency (given the nature of health insurance in the country) and a large-scale market. France represents 4.8% of the global market, the fourth largest market globally, and the second largest in Europe.

3) A favorable ecosystem: according to the international study on clusters of innovation, Paris is ranked tenth, behind seven American cities, Tel Aviv (second in the rankings) and London (which is third). The existence of a favorable ecosystem bringing together the full spectrum of actors (enterprises, universities, research organizations, investors) creates dynamic activity that drives innovations.

4) Public support for Research and Development: this is notably through measures to improve modes of financing research. This is ensured, above all by highly advantageous taxation, with organizations awarded Research Tax Credits.

All these advantages give the innovation market in France a certain edge in the exploration phase. On the other hand, the process of innovation in the exploitation phase does not produce the same results, especially in the healthcare industry. In addition, these innovations are exported to other countries due to the absence of multinational companies in France in this sector, for the exploitation phase. The balance between these two processes is, therefore, not optimal.

Inconsistencies in governance are cited as the cause of the difficulty in optimizing the exploration/exploitation combination. According to the French Court of Auditors, "the public research system does not adequately consider the economic results of research, which are under-accounted for in public spending indicators". And so, for instance, the director of a research laboratory recounts how, in a field which only profits from exploitation, he only has credits available for exploration, which is seen as more valuable to an investor.

On a global scale, inconsistency in the optimization of these two approaches may also be the result of an error at the exploration level: the lack of a way to leverage research or the lack of a key actor such as research organizations, the absence of a favorable ecosystem or, again, the lack of funding to support R&D.

The OECD published a global database in 2016 on the reduced public spending on R&D and the imminent threat to innovation, as seen in the below graph. The report warns against the reduction in state expenses toward R&D, especially in the OECD countries where in 2014, for the first time since they began recording the data in 1981, this expense head showed a decrease.

The following conclusions may be drawn from the OECD report published on 8 December 2016:

– Over a third of the research done globally in government and higher education institutions takes place in non-OECD economies. China spent around twice as much on public R&D as Japan in 2014. India, Russia, Chinese Taipei, Iran and Argentina have some of the world's biggest public science systems.

– Five countries – the USA, China, Japan, Germany and India – accounted for 59% of global public R&D in 2014, while 25 countries were behind 90% of the total. This dominance by a few partly reflects their large size. In the future, economies with fast-growing populations and GDP, as in Africa, may become more important players.

– Charities, foundations and philanthropists have become increasingly prominent funders of university research in recent years, particularly in the area of health where they often fund research into rare or tropical diseases. This will have an impact on future public research agendas.

– Different countries currently have different specializations: for example, health and medical science takes up 24% of public R&D spending in the USA, 22% in the UK and 17% in Canada, while energy R&D is 19% of the total in Mexico, 11% in Japan and 9% in Korea. Country priorities are changing and increasingly reflect the growing societal challenges mentioned above such as climate change and demographics.

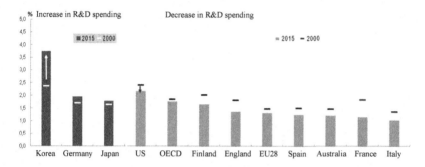

Figure 5.1. *Decreasing public spending on R&D (2000–2015) (source: OECD, Science, Technology and Industry Outlook 2016)*

The warning note struck by the OECD is completely justified. A decrease in public spending on R&D directly affects the state of innovation through exploration. The specter of protectionism pushed the OECD to publish this alert. Given the international context of a backlash against globalization and immigration in certain countries, this only aggravates worries related to knowledge mobility, especially in the field of health. Protectionism does not promote innovation (which depends on public spending) and leads to a decrease in international cooperation, especially in the health sector or healthcare industry.

Thus, across systems, innovation in the field of health through exploration is based on public spending on R&D and on the very long-term allocation of resources. Moreover, these allocations represent one of the principal weaknesses in healthcare organizations' strategies to optimally combine exploitation and exploration, as the incentive system is not compatible with social utility. We thus now turn to study the processes of "growth economics", which may help open up new avenues of thought.

5.3. Using endogenous growth models

The endogenous growth theory offers an analysis model that is based on two simple and fundamental principles. The first: innovation is an endogenous factor that results from investment decisions taken by economic agents. The state first allocates funding for basic research. These resources are then transformed into human capital, which is a key factor in innovation. Organizations then spend on R&D to produce and market new innovations. All this leads to greater economic growth.

The second principle uses Schumpeter's mechanism: the continuous accumulation of knowledge makes it possible to use productive factors more efficiently, which leads to long-term economic growth.

Solow's model [SOL 56] is the starting point for growth models. This theoretician explained economic growth using labor, technical capital (machines, software, etc.) and, above all, technological progress (innovation). Indeed, in Solow's initial model, the growth of technical capital led to an increase in production but not with the same proportion, until a steady state was reached (additional increase in capital corresponds to the moment when rise in production is slower than rise in production costs). Thus, economic growth will slowly reduce until it stops altogether. However, in observed reality, even though growth slowed it continued to take place. To make Solow's model more realistic, we can integrate continuous technical innovations into the theory, which makes it possible to avoid stagnation in production and to stave off the steady state as long as there are new innovations.

Romer [ROM 86] enriched the analysis model by introducing externalities: the investment an organization makes in an innovation will lead to an increase in its production, but it will also increase the production of other organizations who may or may not be competitors. This is explained by the knowledge accumulation that leads to the innovation and that will, inevitably, be diffused to other organizations.

Among the unique features of innovation in the health sector is the length of its life cycle – usually a few weeks to a few months in some sectors. The exploration phase in the field of health requires a much longer timeframe to develop new inventions. This is why the health sector, in particular, has a need for long-term, or even very-long-term, funding.

This funding is considered as risk capital. It is of primordial importance right from the early stage of the development of the innovation, or even of the company, up until the stage of validating clinical tests. Once in this phase, the company or organization may need fresh funding for the marketing of this new innovation. And even when the organization reaches a stage where it is able to self-finance, it may require funding for large-scale product expansion.

Long-term funding for innovations in the health sector is, therefore, an important factor for knowledge accumulation, on the one hand, and for the development of health, on the other. Economic agents, however, do not always all react in the same way when confronted with the need for funding for an innovation. The uncertainty investors face is essentially due to information asymmetry. Before making a choice, investors need to search for information in order to know the true value of the innovations. This search for information involves additional costs for these agents. Furthermore, investment in innovations, especially in the health sector, is made through financial intermediaries.

Let us take the example of biotechnology companies, where the life cycle of medicines is generally very long, and also very expensive, with a unique risk and uncertainty related to the overall economic environment in these companies. This influences the decisions of investors, who cannot see the potential and growth advantages that these new medicines may offer. This step is often called the "startup" stage of the innovation. At this stage, the initial economic strategy model of the company is unstable and must be regularly adjusted. According to Sadi [SAD 14], the investor perceives this model to give poor assurance as to the control of risk and the growth potential of technological projects. This explains why some observers call the "startup" phase of an innovation "the valley of death". This investor perception and the investors' aversion to risk and external financial losses have been reinforced and heightened by the radical technological breakthroughs of the last decade and the current crisis in the healthcare industry, brought about by a fall in innovation, especially radical innovations, as well as the loss of "*blockbusters*".

Continuing with the theme of information asymmetry, another constraint that may affect funding of innovations in the health sector is the motivation among investors, especially the motivation levels of banks, who are the most important actors for loans taken to fund innovations. First, banks look for short-term profitability in their investment, knowing that the exploration process in the health sector requires long-term funding. Second, the fact that banks have a tendency to minimize risks related to their investments, through checks and controls, results in two negative situations as concerns the funding of innovations: banks either overestimate the risk (as banks do not generally have specialized monitoring services) or they are discouraged by the costs of the monitoring required.

The motivation levels of investors determine whether or not an innovation receives funding. This is also true for companies in the healthcare sector who wish to work on an innovation in the exploration phase, within a self-financing framework. These companies meet with the same problem of finding an appropriate balance of economic and social utility in the context of an asymmetry in information.

5.4. Innovation and Corporate Social Responsibility

Social utility must be prioritized for the well-being and good health of individuals. Among the economic trends that have approached this problem, the concept of Corporate Social Responsibility (CSR) opens up new paths to explore.

CSR is defined as a collection of "actions that seem to promote some social good, beyond the company's own interests and what is required by law" [MCW 01]. This allows organizations to develop a vision that goes beyond simply maximizing profits. Proposed in October 2011, the 3rd Communication from the European Commission on the Social Responsibility of corporate entities is a doctrinal summary. It offers the following definition of CSR: "the responsibility of companies vis-à-vis the impact they have on society".

The commission adds: "In order to assume this responsibility, companies must first respect the legislation in vigor and collective conventions concluded between social partners". "In order to discharge their social responsibility to the fullest extent, companies must be engaged in close collaboration with their stakeholders; a process aimed to integrate their concerns on social, environmental, ethical, human rights and consumer issues into the company's commercial activity and basic strategy". "[…] In order to take note of, prevent or attenuate the potential negative effects that they may have, large companies and companies that are particularly exposed to the risk of having negative impacts, are incentivized to demonstrate the diligence required, depending on the risks, including within their supply chain". The communication additionally requires public powers to design a "smart mix" of obligations and incentives to promote CSR.

Implementing CSR may have a positive effect on innovation across health system organizations, especially in overcoming the economic constraints taken into account for the funding of innovation during the exploration stage.

In addition to this, and from the point of view of long-term economics, the responsible approach taken by organizations with continuous innovations will, over time, improve not only the quality of their social goals but also, and most importantly, their economic goals.

This vision of the impact of innovation within the CSR framework is not equally shared within the scientific community and is even less widely shared among directors of companies. As certain authors [HUS 07] point out, CSR is very expensive and offers companies no advantages other than earning good reputation. The authors add that for many CEOs who were interviewed recently about their CSR processes, undertaking a CSR project seemed inevitable, but they were dubious about it resulting in any real value creation for their company.

However, according to the hypothesis proposed by Porter [POR 91], innovation and competitiveness are not necessarily antagonistic. And CSR may stimulate innovation, which could lead to value creation that companies might not have thought of otherwise [POR 95].

Even though Porter's hypothesis is mainly focused on environmental responsibility, this also holds true for responsibility related to public or individual health. This is especially true in today's context of globalization which is quite advantageous to creations and innovations within the health sector.

The question of the governance of CSR and of public intervention within the legal framework that promotes CSR in companies is essential in order to obtain the expected results according to Porter's theory. This is because economic utility predominates when making investment decisions or the decision to fund innovation projects in the field of healthcare. However, it is generally social utility that prevails in the improvement of health and well-being. Even though the long-term economic impacts may be large, from a macro-dynamic point of view, this does not greatly encourage organizations or financiers to invest in innovations in the exploration phase, as they are more motivated to look for short-term profits. Public intervention to encourage CSR could have a positive impact on the funding for innovations in the exploration phase.

5.5. Connected health and integrated care

The European countries that are the most advanced in terms of connected health are also countries where integrated health service programs have been promoted for a long time. These are essentially the Scandinavian countries. Recent legislative provisions were introduced to German and French law on health (2016) to prevent the widening of the gap between the most advanced countries and other European countries. The synergy between the coordination of care in integrated health services and connected health is based on four aspects:

– Better coordination between Research and Application: for instance, researchers may be offered incentives to publish in "starred" journals, which only accept approaches that are far from any application. While the transgenic mouse model may be a very good way of getting published, it also inadequate for developing any application, which results in a complete disconnect between exploration and exploitation.

– Building on technologies with a shorter cycle than the one hampering the health sector. German law calls for projects that promote better coordination between care services and incentivizes more dynamic management of innovation, especially for exploitation.

– Integrated health services initiate incremental innovations in the exploitation approach and encourage high-quality policies in health organizations, which is not possible in the solitary or isolated practice of the general practitioner.

– Integrated health services seek to unify multiple actors around a common professional ethic. The institutionalist approach, traditionally based on the reinforcement of property rights, does not lead to improvements in the innovation cycle and has a negative role in multiplying the effects of working in isolation.

6

Healthcare Networks

For about 30 years now, there has been great progress in research and analysis into the functioning of health systems using tools and concepts from pure economics. Thus, many theories have contributed to studies in the field of health economics and to renewed interest in the vision of health and its problems in economics. For example, making use of the agency theory to help make health policy decisions, or again, organizational theories when searching for modes of coordination within the health system.

More recently, over the past few years, a new stream of literature has emerged. The authors of this branch of literature propose the use of the concept of networks in the economic analysis of health systems. This new concept has been met with great success within scientific and political communities around the world.

In this chapter, we will first define the concept of healthcare networks through a brief historical study of the emergence of these networks, and then examine how this concept could be pertinent when discussing improvements in healthcare and its organization. We will then study the relationship between healthcare networks and the contemporary human demand for a longer life and better health, within the framework of citizenship and associated rights. Finally, we will try to get a broad overview of the contributions of different economic theories to the analysis of health networks.

6.1. Defining healthcare networks: their history and development

Until 4 March 2002, France had no official definition for a healthcare network. However, on this date, the formal definition was included in the French Public Health Code, in article L6321-1, which reads, "The objective of healthcare networks is to promote access to healthcare, coordination, continuity or an interdisciplinary approach in providing healthcare, especially healthcare specific to certain populations, pathologies or health activities. These networks ensure that appropriate care is provided, depending on the needs of the individual, whether these needs relate to health education, prevention, diagnosis or to the provision of care. These networks may participate in public health actions. They carry out evaluations in order to guarantee the quality of the services they offer."

In order to better understand this definition, we must go back to the origin of the concept of a healthcare network. This concept first appeared in the aftermath of the HIV/AIDS outbreak, which caused great concern throughout the population that faced the risk of contamination, among healthcare professionals who were confronted with the impotence of therapeutics in the face of this illness and health authorities concerned over public health. Indeed, health systems were found to be completely incapable of finding a solution to this situation.

Patients with AIDS would take the help of different organizations to claim their right to learn about, and to participate in, their own care. Healthcare professionals responded positively, in the sense that they were willing to re-examine routine hierarchies and to actively participate in this network. The long-term care for those affected in the HIV/AIDS pandemic corresponds in reality to many patient profiles that have changed, especially in developed countries where we are seeing an ageing population and a more widespread management of chronic pathologies that require more adapted care over a longer period.

Thus, healthcare networks were born out of the initiative taken by associations and healthcare professionals who wished to bring in better quality care for their patients. The first real signs that these healthcare networks were succeeding were seen during the heat wave of 2003 (which caused over 70,000 deaths in Europe), when it was noticed that individuals who were cared for within a healthcare network were able to cope with the crisis. Indeed, according to François Frégeac and Emmanuelle Pion [FRE 05], "senior citizens who benefited from being cared for within healthcare networks had lower mortality rates, near-zero, during the heat wave."

The earliest healthcare networks, those in the field of AIDS or in gerontology, for example, were created in order to overcome a deficiency within the health system. However, today, there is such high need for them across many fields that the number of healthcare networks has skyrocketed.

Based on Patte's typology [PAT 98], we can establish four dynamic areas of interest around which the healthcare networks were structured:

– professionals organize themselves into groups to form networks of complementarity and communication;

– financers (health insurance, in particular) aim to develop efficient networks by putting in place forfeits or global envelopes for cover;

– users seek effective help for shared concerns (AIDS, Alzheimer's disease, etc.), if any, by trying to get professionals to structure themselves by forming referral networks;

– territorial collectivities intervene more when it concerns social priorities (homecare for senior citizens, social assistance, etc.) and propose service networks.

Thus, care networks came up to contribute solutions wherever the health system was unable to find appropriate responses to certain crises such as the AIDS crisis, isolated senior citizens facing a heat wave, providing care to people with multiple pathologies, etc.

At the same time as this change was taking place, economists all over the world were reflecting on the contours of "managed care". This is because the efficient functioning of networks is dependent on the managerial principle of coordination between health professionals, the associative sector, the public sector and establishments in the market sector. The main goal that all these bodies set is dependent on both the health economy (as it is, above all, economic) and citizenship (striving for better quality care and support for patients).

For example, in France, according to the documents of the Coordination Nationale des Réseaux (National Coordination of Networks), "Dating from the circular DHOS 88 of 2 March 2007, the objectives of the networks have been reoriented as follows:

Healthcare networks must, in the future, be incentivized to develop a service offering based on the following points: offering professional support so they may refer their patients within the care systems and allow them access to the most appropriate cares. These are classified as:

– resource healthcare professionals;

– referral hospital services;

– services that may, if needed, provide non-reimbursable care or services, not covered by health insurance (chiropractors–podiatrists, psychologists, dietitians, etc.) and offer a similar support to patients and patient associations..."

National Allocation to Networks is confirmed in its vocation of financing certain acts under the term "exempt from tariffs" and of evaluating the necessity of maintaining reimbursements for these acts:

"The exemption from tariffs mentioned in article L.162-45 of the French Social Security Code must remain experimental, that is, with a limited timeframe and level of remuneration. These services, whose efficiency or therapeutic value have been proven, are meant to become Common law services in order to avoid any iniquity in access to care between patients and any positioning of the network on modes of competition vis-à-vis other health service providers. An exemption from tariffs must meet at least one of the following criteria:

– the non-identification of the concerned act or provision in nomenclature;

– the necessity for the intervention of several professionals from different professions;

– the absence of any convention between the interventionist who provides the service and the Health Insurance;

– the non-presence of a patient when the act is carried out (for example, a multidisciplinary consultation).

The request for exemptions must increase depending on referrals from existing practices and, right from the experimental phase, they must measure the financial impact to be expected from their eventual generalization."

Before we delve into the question of healthcare networks in the health economy, let us look at the improvements that the healthcare networks could bring about in patient care, in the context of the evolution of present-day society.

6.2. Care networks and citizenship

Human society today aspires to a longer lifespan, to live in the best health conditions possible. The human development index exists to remind us that in advanced societies, intangible assets and conditions of social development are the most important objectives across the society. Institutions must adapt themselves to these societal imperatives. From a historical point of view, never before, from the earliest civilizations, has society procured so many rights for patients.

As indicated above, the care networks emerged to respond to just this need, to offer patients a coordinated response across their care and support, with the most appropriate quality for each type of pathology, and to thus participate in improving the care provided to patients. The question that we can ask of ourselves is: how do healthcare networks contribute in responding to this citizen demand?

In the logic of the emerging healthcare networks, the important problem was to overcome the notorious information asymmetry that was inherent to the health system. On the one hand, we have health professionals with medical and administrative know-how, and on the other hand, we have patients who have no medical knowledge concerning their pathologies and who are drowning in administrative paperwork.

In this case, the support they offer care networks greatly helps patients and their caregivers, providing information about their diseases and helping them find the services they need. This was the case with the AIDS patient networks, for example, or the cancer networks, which have brought about much wider recognition of the physical and psychological sufferings of the patients, as well as helping in furthering understanding of their treatment, which cannot be condensed into a simple therapeutic protocol. Another important consideration is that there are individuals who may not aspire for good health, but at least live with dignity, and thus have the right to information.

The care networks also provide a solution to the isolated state that many patients find themselves in, by organizing complementary activities such as group meetings, meetings with healthcare professionals or social assistance professionals through training programs, none of which they could have without being part of a network. This is especially true for chronic pathologies, where patients are more or less held captive in the care system for a longer period, and sometimes, until the end of their lives as is the case with cancer, AIDS or neurodegenerative diseases. This captivity is often episodic. Patients then find themselves outside the hospital setting, and since they are no longer cared for by the hospital, this is where care networks intervene. We can cite here the example of care networks in the field of gerontology, which developed the earliest logical framework for these networks to cope with difficulties related to caring for dependent senior citizens. This is because in modern societies, we are witnessing a dismantling of social and familial networks, which earlier used to care for the aged in the family residence and would, more or less, provide all the care required out of the hospital. Today's care networks organize social support.

6.3. Healthcare networks and health economics

The concept of a network is very widely used in many research disciplines (physics, informatics, economy, sociology). This concept has met with such success that we find a variety of concepts within the same discipline. In economics, we come across this concept in the analysis of distribution networks, migration networks and working networks. We also speak of networks of a technical nature, such as telecommunications or in research on health economics focused on care networks.

The concept of a "network" covers many approaches in economics. One approach defines a network as a structure of economic activities. Another approach defines it as a modality of coordination, an alternative to the market as a mode of allocation of resources. In health economics, the approach used to analyze the network consists of considering it as being a mode of coordination that is an alternative to the market, contracts or conventions. It must be noted here that many theories have developed around coordination within the health system, such as, the agency theory, the transactional costs theory, organizational theories, convention theory, network theory, evolutionary economics, etc.

In this book, we will refer to three principal theories, which define coordination within the context of care networks. We will first examine the agency theory, applied to health and to healthcare networks. We will then look at the application of the convention theory to the field of health. We will finally study the evolutionary and socio-economic approach to care networks.

6.3.1. *The agency theory as applied to healthcare networks*

According to Sebai [SEB 16], applying the agency theory (AT) to health systems makes it possible to highlight the conflicts of interest, the information asymmetries, and the risks associated with economic activities in relations between agents. The concerned agents in our work may belong to any type of care network in a region.

The AT [JEN 76] analyzes the relationship in which the principal (who can delegate decision-making power) delegates his power of choice to another person, the agent or proxy. This is a relationship of coordination where the principal must draw up a contract incentivizing the agent to share the risks associated with the delegation, while also trying to avoid the agent exercising opportunistic strategies.

The most important element in the AT is the information asymmetry between the principal, who has no information, and the agent, who holds all the information. Sebai [SEB 16] identifies three types of information asymmetry as related to the relationships of agency in the context of the structure of coordinated care:

– between authorities (the principal) and structures (the agent) mainly in the case of distortions in allocations and endowments where the interests of the principal run contrary to those of the agent;

– between the doctor or healthcare professionals (the principal) and the patient (the agent) where the information asymmetry forces the patient to delegate power to the principal;

– between the doctor (the principal) and the nurse (the agent), the information asymmetry is less significant than in the preceding category.

Thus, in healthcare networks, information asymmetry in the context of the AT represents the complete set of relationships that connect the different actors in these networks and the health professionals.

The principal/agent model here is based on the agents' endogenous behavior. The coordination relations use incentivizing methods in order to avoid opportunistic behaviors that may impair coordination and reduce the effectiveness of the cooperation. This is the case with the funding for the European Union, for example, with the funding being allocated based on the criteria of investment in, and access to, healthcare for patients, in research on rare diseases or based on the contribution to innovation in health.

The incentive mechanism in AT in the case of the analysis of care networks must be discussed more cautiously. This is because the objective of the use of incentives, through additional revenues, endowments or allocations under this theory, is to prevent opportunistic behavior. In addition, collective coordination at the level of the care networks already exists, and financial compensations to the networks alone would not explain why this coordination works.

In the case of healthcare networks, we can consider two other scenarios for this:

– there is good coordination in healthcare networks, and in this case, incentive mechanisms may lead to opportunistic behaviors;

– a large drop in financial contributions may impair the functioning of collective coordination.

The AT as applied to care networks does not take into consideration the collective cooperation between the different actors. However, the agent's interests in this theory's analysis are primarily built on individual relations. In addition to this, and among the other properties of the agent as per the AT, there is the fact that the agent's behavior is rational and calculating. When it comes to health networks, the agent is not necessarily endowed with these behaviors given the nature and specific features of the relations between the different agents in the network. Thus, for example, the rationality of agents is not infinite. It is even limited, if we take into account the large quantity of information and continuous flux of therapeutic and medical innovations. Agents (health professionals) can never have all the information available to them at all times, even in spite of wide experience. Agents also do not have the capacity for the calculation required to select the optimal decision (no information asymmetry, no non-probability risk, etc.).

6.3.2. *The convention theory as applied to healthcare networks*

The convention theory is an interesting theory to apply to healthcare networks as it tries to introduce sociological considerations to economic analysis, which the AT lacked. This theory seeks to identify the coordination mechanisms that economic agents use to adjust their decisions in a decentralized environment (not regulated by a central authority).

Among the contributions this theory has made, with respect to the AT, we can list three interesting elements that can be included in the analysis of the coordination of care networks: the heterogeneity of agents, convention as a relative construction, and the nature of the collective.

– The heterogeneity of agents makes it possible to highlight the existence of real coordination problems in the analysis. This means that agents that make up the actors in the health network are different, with contradictory interests. This forces the agents to cooperate despite their different positions, as being the only solution to these contradictions. Salais [SAL 89] describes this: "The convention is a form that makes it possible to coordinate contradictory interests that arise from opposing rationales but which need to be brought together in order to be satisfied."

– A convention is considered to be a relative construct, built around individual actions that result in a process of general consistency across these actions. The convention is, thus, a dynamic process whose analysis is focused on the problem of what makes up the convention, its duration, and above all, the coordination and not the general equilibrium brought in by coordination in neoclassical theory. This implies that a convention X exists in order to provide a solution to a coordination problem Y.

– Contrary to the methodological individualism in AT, a convention admits the collective nature of agreements between agents. The theory is that these agreements must have a common and collective framework of interpretation for individual actions, so that their executions are compatible between themselves. According to Favereau [FAV 89], conventions or rules may thus be defined as collective cognitive tools. The fundamentals of this approach highlight the importance of confidence and the motivation of agents in the coordination of individual actions that have a common objective. The concept of organization thus becomes a weaving together of inter-individual relations in a collective logic.

These three properties are interesting in our case of the analysis of coordination in care networks. This is particularly true when it comes to the non-commercial aspect of our subject of study, as coordination relations between agents in the field of health (healthcare professionals/patients/associations/other actors in the network) are carried out such that the economic aspect does not predominate, but rather is inserted into the social aspect. This altruistic dimension and the collective aspect of the engagement, as well as the professional ethics of this field, promote the coordination of collaborative relations that are based on confidence between the heterogeneous agents. This confidence is also the basic structure used to explain this coordination through the evolutionary theory.

6.3.3. *The evolutionary and socio-economic approach to care networks*

In the evolutionary approach, agents in a care network find themselves in a situation where uncertainty over the future is directly linked to innovation in the field of health, whether therapeutic, medical, biotechnological or social. In this context of uncertainty, evolutionary theory considers that the coordination interactions between agents in the healthcare network are a source of learning, of information and knowledge-sharing, and the cause for changes or adjustment in the behavior of the actors in the network.

According to Coriat and Weinstein [COR 95], coordination between actors in the context of the evolutionary theory cannot take place without the confidence factor. Furthermore, as stated above, this is similar to the analysis carried out using the convention theory. As Sebai [SEB 16] emphasizes, "Strong similarities must be pointed out between the conventional and the evolutionary approach. The additional contribution that evolutionary theory brings in terms of resource creation is due to its deeper examination of the subject, as it is especially interested in the problem of the coordination of resources and by the resources within the structures as well as between different organizations and stakeholders (actors: healthcare professionals, medico-social workers, care institutions (regional health agencies), public organizations (general counsel, at the level of the *Département*), etc." Evolutionary theory tries to analyze how coordination in the context of confident collaboration between actors in a healthcare network leads to knowledge creation.

In addition to this aspect of confidence, we can identify two other contributions of the evolutionary theory that seem relevant to the analysis of coordination within care networks:

1) *The desire to reduce uncertainties:* The health field is characterized by uncertainty over the future relating to two broad points: (1) uncertainty related to iatrogenic risk factors for the patient, who find themselves in a position of uncertainty when confronted with treatments that the medical corps propose; (2) uncertainty of the medical professional (expert) when faced with the perpetual transformation of medical knowledge as a result of technological and therapeutic innovation, which often changes knowledge available on the pathology. According to Dosi [DOS 88], to reduce the uncertainties related to decisions, the constitution of the healthcare

network makes it possible for an informal platform to emerge. This becomes the meeting point for different points of view and experiences that promote the establishment of routines, norms, or yet again, behaviors.

2) *Coordination as the origin of creation and of the diffusion of knowledge:* the very existence of a care network and a willingness to collaborate enables the diffusion of information. The accumulation of information and scattered knowledge leads to the creation of new knowledge and new competencies. For example, the existence of a care network for breast cancer implies the specialization of several actors who participate in the treatment and follow-up process for the disease. This is how new skills specific to this disease are created. With this care network and in order to meet patients' need for psychological support, new skills and knowledge were developed within the field of psychology. Thus, today we find psycho-oncologists[1], specialized in helping patients with breast cancer. This is despite the fact that most psychologists have not received theoretical training in the specific psychological aspects related to breast cancer. The contribution of each intervening specialist in the network leads to the growth of knowledge among other actors through learning mechanisms. In this example, continuity in psychological support is very important in the treatment of the illness. However, this would not be possible unless the psycho-oncologists shared their knowledge and experience in the context of collaboration between different actors in the care protocol. Similarly, as concerns the inter-hospital cooperation relations, cooperation that is set up as a means of forming more links allows for a pooling of knowledge and know-how, a source that leads to the development of individual and collective skills through learning.

Changes to health systems that no longer respond to the needs of modern-day society come in via the creation of care networks, at a time when humans, through citizen demands, are seeking to live longer, in good health or with the best possible care to live with

---

1 Psychologists trained to offer support in the field of cancer.

dignity. With this concept of network, we must redefine the coordination of relationships between the different actors. Different approaches from different economic theories contribute in a complementary manner to the coordination of the decisions taken by agents. Contrary to neo-classical theory, convention and evolutionary theories allow us to bring in the social field, which is very important when analyzing the field of health. In addition to the aspect of confidence as a factor in the coordination of actors in a healthcare network, as in conventional theory, evolutionary theory tries to reduce the uncertainties around the decisions taken by agents. This approach allows us to also better understand the creation of resources through learning mechanisms and through the diffusion of information.

6.3.4. *From the specific to the universal: medical deserts and multiple pathologies*

Care networks have evolved such that people-centered integrated health services have emerged as a prominent theme. The transformation dynamics was based on several elements: on the one hand, norms introduce an evolution toward universal coverage, as has already been the law in France, for example, since 2002. Behaviors that group sub-populations around a pathology are basically antithetical to the general principles of equity that govern the regulatory framework. Other dynamic elements are practical in nature. An individual often suffers from several pathologies, and therefore a pathology-specific approach will be inadequate: patients being treated for one illness will be in danger from another illness that has not been treated or is under-treated. On the service offerings dimension, the earliest care networks were often defined as filling in a secondary gap in a medical specialization – if this specialization were part of a network, it would cut down the waiting list for each specialist. However, a large part of the world's population (about 20% of the population of the USA, as per 2013 statistics) lives in a medical desert. The experience of integrated care networks in China may be explained by a hospital-centered health system [SHI 15]. The problems here concern providing care to a rural population that presents long-term ailments – the inadequacy of health services are not limited to a specific pathology, but are widespread and affect different pathologies. Other issues have come up from this change, such as, managing any stigma and possible discrimination toward sick people or the disabled. Populations may be reluctant to participate in prevention and screening campaigns for TB in sub-Saharan Africa, due to the comorbidity of TB and AIDS. This leads to the establishment of pediatric-obstetric healthcare networks that also treat communicable diseases [FOW 16]. Specific WHO programs target countries where qualified personnel are concentrated at a single geographical location. The universal policy of a healthcare network is determined by the problem of decentralization, starting from an agglomeration effect among health personnel.

Conclusion

A Global Report

Integrated person-centered health services formulate a global program for a health system. This program is a process based on the organizational gains that accompany transformations in pathologies, technologies and organizations in the field of health. The 2015–2030 Sustainable Development Goals, fixed by the international community, are not very ambitious as regards goals for the field of health, although they do affirm the general principles of reducing health inequalities. Organizational transformations will be essential for effective progress made in healthcare across the world.

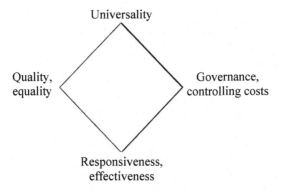

Figure 1. *Recapitulative table for aspects of a health system [PAL 12]*

Quality of care, increasing the number of people with guaranteed healthcare, cost control, cutting delays and waiting lists – all of these are legitimate provisions that populations can expect from the health system. To evaluate the performance of health systems, these expectations are distributed over different indicators, lying along independent axes (see Figure 1).

The context for these reforms in the field of health is not marked by a normative procedure that can satisfy all these expectations with a single, unified approach. Referring to, and drawing from, the major health systems across history can only fulfill a few of these expectations. The principal flaws in each of these systems are known: waiting lists, in the Beveridgean system; problems of governance and cutting costs in the Bismarckian system; and mediocre quality and poor responsiveness in systems based on the Alma-Alta model.

Figure 2. *Quality policies and types of health systems*

Reducing health inequalities has several dimensions: financial, spatial and behavioral. Spatial inequalities, for instance, are ubiquitous, such as medical deserts on all continents, at different levels (zonal, regional, and continental). All across the world, we see the same mechanism underlying agglomeration, depriving rural zones of doctors (all doctors remain in the city). This can be solved through integrated care policies – the only possible way of achieving the Sustainable Development Goals and the goals of ensuring quality and equality in healthcare [WHI 16].

Bibliography

[ABS 07] ABSI P., PHELINAS P., SELIM M., "Hommes et femmes face aux inégalités et à la pauvreté au travail", in BAUMANN E., BAZIN L., OULD-AHMED P. *et al.* (eds), *La mondialisation au risque des travailleurs*, L'Harmattan, Paris, 2007.

[BAR 14] BARNETT J.H., LEWIS L., BLACKWELL A.D. *et al.*, "Early intervention in Alzheimer's disease: a health economic study of the effects of diagnostic timing", *BMC Neurology*, vol. 14, no. 1, pp. 1–19, 2014.

[BLA 82] BLACK D., *Inequalities in Health: The Black Report*, Penguin Books, New York, 1982.

[BLO 15] BLOY G., "Echec des messages préventifs et gouvernement des conduites en médecine générale", *Sciences sociales et santé*, vol. 33, no. 4, pp. 41–66, 2015.

[BRA 04] BRAUMAN R., "Article 'Humanitaire'", in LECOURT D. (ed.), *Dictionnaire de la pensée médicale*, PUF, Paris, 2004.

[BRA 09] BRAUMAN R., *La médecine humanitaire*, PUF, Paris, 2009.

[CAM 08] CAMBOIS E., LABORDE C., ROBINE J.-M., "La 'double peine' des ouvriers: plus d'années d'incapacité au sein d'une vie plus courte", *Population et sociétés*, no. 441, INED, Paris, January 2008.

[CAM 92] CAMERER C., WEBER M., "Recent developments in modeling preferences: uncertainty and ambiguity", *Journal of Risk and Uncertainty*, vol. 5, pp. 325–370, 1992.

[CAR 15] CARR A.R., PAHOLPAK P., DAIANU M. *et al.*, "An investigation of care-based vs. rule-based morality in frontotemporal dementia, Alzheimer's disease, and healthy controls", *Neuropsychologia*, vol. 78, pp. 73–79, 2015.

[CAU 00] CAUVIN J., *La naissance de l'agriculture*, Éditions du CNRS, Paris, 2000.

[CHA 05] CHAUVIN P., PARIZOT I., *Santé et recours aux soins des populations vulnérables*, Editions Inserm, Paris, 2005.

[CHE 13] CHEN R., HU Z., CHEN R.L. *et al.*, "Determinants for undetected dementia and late-life depression", *The British Journal of Psychiatry*, vol. 203, no. 3, pp. 203–208, 2013.

[COL 08] COLLIER P., *The bottom billion: Why the poorest countries are failing and what can be done about it*, Oxford University Press, New York, 2008.

[CON 01] CONTANDRIOPOULOS A.-P., DENIS J.-L., TOUATI N. *et al.*, "Intégration des soins: dimensions et mise en œuvre", *Ruptures. Revue transdisciplinaire en santé*, vol. 8, no. 2, pp. 38–52, 2001.

[COR 95] CORIAT B., WEINSTEIN O., *Les nouvelles théories de la firme*, Le Livre de Poche, Paris, 1995.

[COR 13] CORVOL A., *Valeurs, attitudes et pratiques des gestionnaires de cas en gérontologie. Une éthique professionnelle en construction*, Descartes, Paris, 2013.

[COT 15] COTLEAR D. *et al.*, "Overcoming social segregation in health care in Latin America", *The Lancet*, vol. 385, pp. 1248–1259, March 2015.

[CRO 77] CROZIER M., FRIEDBERG E., *L'acteur et le système: les contraintes de l'action collective*, Le Seuil, Paris, 1977.

[COU 05] COUFFINHAL A., DOURGNON P., GEOFFRAD P.Y. *et al.*, "Politiques de réduction des inégalités de santé, quelle place pour le système de santé? Un éclairage européen", *Questions d'économie de la santé*, nos. 92–93, Irdes, February 2005.

[CUT 08] CUTLER D.M., LLERAS-MUNEY A., VOGL T., Socio economic status and health: dimensions and mechanisms, NBER Working Paper, no. 14333, 2008.

[DAN 05] DANDURANT L., "Réflexion autour du concept d'innovation sociale, approche historique et comparative", *Revue française d'administration publique*, 2005/3. N, vol. 115, pp. 377–382, 2005.

[DAV 01] DAVIS M., *Late Victorian Holocausts: El Nino Famines and the Making of the Third World*, Verso, London-New York, 2001.

[DEA 13] DEATON A., *The Great Escape: Health, Wealth, and the Origins of Inequality*, Princeton University Press, 2013.

[DIA 97] DIAMOND J., *De l'inégalité parmi les sociétés*, Gallimard, Paris, 1997.

[DIE 01] DIEZ-ROUX A., "Investigating neighbourhood and area effect on health", *American Journal of Public Health*, vol. 91, no. 11, pp. 1783–1789, 2001.

[DOI 88] DOI T., *Le jeu de l'indulgence* (French translation), L'Asiathèque, Paris, 1988.

[DOS 88] DOSI G., "Sources, procedures, and microeconomic effects of innovation", *Journal of Economic Literature*, vol. 26, pp. 1120–1171, 1988.

[FAN 04] FAN R., LI B., "Truth telling in medicine: the Confucian view", *The Journal of Medicine and Philosophy*, vol. 29, no. 2, pp. 179–193, 2004.

[FAN 11] FAN R., "The Confucian bioethics of surrogate decision making: its communitarian roots", *Theoretical Medicine and Bioethics*, vol. 32, no. 5, pp. 301–313, 2011.

[FAV 89] FAVEREAU O., Marchés internes, marchés externes, *Revue économique*, vol. 40, no. 2, pp. 273–328, March 1989.

[FES 64] FESTINGER L., *Conflict, Decision and Dissonance*, Stanford University Press, Stanford, 1964.

[FOU 63] FOUCAULT M., *Naissance de la Clinique*, PUF, Paris, 1963.

[FOW 16] FOWKES F., DRAPER B., HELLARD M. *et al.*, "Achieving development goals for HIV, tuberculosis and malaria in sub-Saharan Africa through integrated antenatal care: barriers and challenges", *BMC Medicine*, vol. 14, p. 202, 2016.

[FRE 05] FREGEAC F., PION E., "Les réseaux gérontologiques MSA: un bilan positif aujourd'hui reconnu", *Technologie & Santé*, 2005.

[GAN 06] GANZACH Y., "Judging risk and return of financial assets", *Organizational Behavior and Human Decision Processes*, vol. 83, no. 2, pp. 353–370, 2006.

[GRI 16] GRIMALDI A., "Quel avenir du système de santé? Le probable et le possible", *Attac*, no. 10, 2016.

[HAR 94] HARRIS P., MIDDLETON W., "The illusion of control and optimism about health: on being less at risk but no more in control than others", *British Journal of Social Psychology*, vol. 33, pp. 369–386, 1994.

[HEA 95] HEATON J., "An empirical investigation of asset pricing with temporally dependent preference specifications", *Econometrica*, vol. 63, pp. 681–717, 1995.

[HUS 07] HUSTED B.W., ALLEN D.B., "Strategic corporate social responsibility and value creation among large firms: lessons from the Spanish experience", *Long Range Planning*, vol. 40, no. 6, pp. 594–610, 2007.

[JEN 76] JENSEN M.C., MECKLING W.H., "Theory of the firm: managerial behavior, agency costs and ownership structure", *Journal of Financial Economics*, vol. 3, no. 4, pp. 305–360, 1976.

[KAH 82] KAHNEMAN D., SLOVIC P., TVERSKY A., *Judgment under Uncertainty: Heuristics and Biases*, Cambridge University Press, Cambridge, 1982.

[KAH 83] KAHNEMAN D., TVERSKY A., "Judgment under uncertainty: heuristics and biases", *Science*, vol. 185, pp. 1124–1131, 1983.

[KAH 92] KAHNEMAN D., TVERSKY A., "Advances in prospect theory: Cumulative representation of uncertainty", *Journal of Risk and Uncertainty*, vol. 5, no. 4, pp. 297–323, 1992.

[KAH 96] KAHNEMAN D., TVERSKY A., "On the reality of cognitive illusions", *Psychological Review*, vol. 103, pp. 582–591, 1996.

[KIH 84] KIHLSTROM J.F., CANTOR N., "Mental representations of the self", in BERKOWITZ L. (ed.), *Advances in Experimental Social Psychology*, vol. 17, Academic Press, New York, 1984.

[KOU 06] KOUABENAN D.R., CADET B., HERMAND D., *Psychologie du risque: Identifier, évaluer, prévenir*, De Boeck, Brussels, 2006.

[KOU 15] KOUDIATI *et al.*, "Child Health services in Burkina Faso: Quality of care and equity in utilization", *9th European Congress on Tropical Medicine*, Basel, Switzerland, 2015.

[KRU 66] KRUGMAN P., "A model of innovation, technology transfer, and the world distribution of income", *Journal of International Economics*, November 1966.

[KU 16] KU L.E., PAI M., SHIH P., "Economic impact of dementia by disease severity: exploring the relationship between stage of dementia and cost of care in Taiwan", *Plos One*, vol. 11, no. 2, pp. 1–12, 2016.

[LE 15] LE GALES C., BUNGENER M. *et al.*, *Alzheimer: Préserver ce qui importe. Les capabilités dans l'accompagnement à domicile*, PUR, Rennes, 2015.

[LEE 95] LEE S.H.V., JOB R.F.S., "The effect of information on optimism bias", in KENNY D.T., JOB R.F.S. (eds), *Australia's Adolescents: A Health Psychology Perspective*, University of New England Press, Armidale, 1995.

[LEI 09] LEIGH A., JENCKS C., SMEEDING T.M., "Health and economic inequality", in SALVERDA W., NOLAN B., SMEEDING T.M. (eds), *The Oxford Handbook of Economic Inequality*, Oxford University Press, Oxford, 2009.

[LEU 07] LEUNG C., LAM T.H., CHAN W.M. *et al.*, "Lower risk of tuberculosis in obesity", *Archives of Internal Medicine*, vol. 167, pp. 1297–304, 2007.

[LIN 15] LIN S.-K., TSAI Y.-T., LAI J.-N. *et al.*, "Demographic and medication characteristics of traditional Chinese medicine users among dementia patients in Taiwan: a nationwide database study", *Journal of Ethnopharmacology*, vol. 161, pp. 108–115, 2015.

[LIU 12] LIU J., WANG L., TIAN J., "Recognition of dementia in Ancient China", *Neurobiology of Aging*, vol. 33, pp. 2948.e11–2948.e13, 2012.

[MAC 08] MACKENBACH J.P., STIRBU I., ROSKAM A.J.R. *et al.*, "The European Union Working Group on Socioeconomic Inequalities in Health, Socioeconomic inequalities in health in 22 european countries", *The New England Journal of Medicine*, vol. 358, no. 23, pp. 2468–2481, 2008.

[MAR 91] MARCH J.G., "Exploration and exploitation in organizational learning", *Organization Science*, vol. 2, no. 1, pp. 71–87, 1991.

[MAR 01] MARMOT M., WILKINSON R., "Psychosocial and material pathway in the relation between income and health: a response to Lynch *et al.*", *British Medical Journal*, vol. 322, pp. 1233–1236, 2001.

[MCW 01] MCWILLIAMS A., SIEGEL D., "Corporate social responsibility: a theory of the firm perspective", *Academy of Management Review*, vol. 26, no. 1, pp. 117–127, 2001.

[MIN 79] MINTZBERG H., *The Structuring of Organization. A Synthesis of the Research*, Prentice-Hall, Englewood Cliffs, 1979.

[MIN 16] MINKMAN M.M.N., "Values and principles of integrated care", *International Journal of Integrated Care*, vol. 16, no. 1, p. 2, 2016.

[MOA 93] MOATTI J.-P., BELTZER N., DAB W., "Les modèles d'analyse des comportements à risque face à l'infection à VIH: une conception trop étroite de la rationalité", *Population*, vol. 48, pp. 1505–1534, 1993.

[MÜH 16] MÜHLBACHER A., JOHNSON F.R., YANG J.C. *et al.*, "Do you want to hear the bad news? The value of diagnostic tests for Alzheimer's disease", *Value in Health*, vol. 19, no. 1, pp. 66–74, 2016.

[NAK 14] NAKANISHI M., NAKASHIMA T., "Features of the Japanese national dementia strategy in comparison with international dementia policies: how should a national dementia policy interact with the public health – and social-care systems?", *Alzheimer and Dementia*, vol. 10, pp. 468–476, 2014.

[NOR 86] NOREM J.K., CANTOR N., "Anticipatory and post-hoc cushioning strategies: optimism and defensive pessimism in "risky" situations", *Cognitive Therapy and Research*, vol. 10, pp. 347–362, 1986.

[NUS 12] NUSSBAUM M.C., *Capabilités*, Flammarion, Paris, 2012.

[OEC 05] OECD, Manuel d'Oslo. Principes directeurs pour le recueil et l'interprétation des données sur l'innovation, 3rd ed., DOI: 101787/9789264013124-fr, Paris, 2005.

[OGI 07] OGIEN R., *L'éthique aujourd'hui. Maximalistes et minimalistes*, Gallimard, Paris, 2007.

[OGI 11] OGIEN R., "Les tendances moralistes et inégalitaires de l'éthique du *care*", *Travail, genre et sociétés*, vol. 2, no. 26, pp. 179–182, 2011.

[OLI 15] OLIVIER DE SARDAN J.-P. *et al.*, "Local sustainability and scaling up for user fee exemptions: medical NGOs vis-à-vis health systems", *BMC Health Services Research*, vol. 15, no. Suppl 3, p. S5, 2015.

[PAL 12] PALIER B., *La réforme des systèmes de santé*, 6th ed., PUF, Paris, 2012.

[PAT 98] PATTE D., "Les réseaux et la santé publique", *La Revue ADSP*, vol. 24, pp. 15–17, 1998.

[PEE 97] PEETERS G., CAMMAERT M.-F., CZAPINSKY J., "Unrealistic optimism and positive/negative asymmetry: a conceptual and cross-cultural study of interrelations between optimism, pessimism and realism", *International Journal of Psychology*, vol. 32, pp. 23–34, 1997.

[PER 86] PERLOFF L.S., FETZER B.K., "Self-other judgments and perceived vulnerability to victimization", *Journal of Personality and Social Psychology*, vol. 50, pp. 502–510, 1986.

[PHI 01] PHILIPSON T.J., "The world-wide growth in obesity: an economic research agenda", *Health Economics*, vol. 10, pp. 1–7, 2001.

[PHI 03] PHILIPSON T.J., POSNER R.A., "The long run growth in obesity as a function of technological change", *Perspectives in Biology and Medicine*, vol. 46, no. 3, pp. 87–107, 2003.

[POR 91] PORTER M.E., "Towards a dynamic theory of strategy", *Strategic Management Journal*, vol. 12, no. S2, pp. 95–117, 1991.

[POR 95] PORTER M.E., VAN DER LINDE C., "Toward a new conception of the environment-competitiveness relationship", *The Journal of Economic Perspectives*, vol. 9, no. 4, pp. 97–118, 1995.

[PUR 07] PURI M., ROBINSON D.T., "Optimism and economic choice", *Journal of Financial Economics*, vol. 86, no. 1, pp. 71–99, 2007.

[RAW 08] RAWLS J., *La justice comme équité*, La Découverte, Paris, 2008.

[RAY 15] RAYNAUD J., *Inégalités d'accès aux soins*, Economica, Paris, 2015.

[REN 94] RENFREW C., MIECH-CHATENAY M., *L'énigme indo-européenne: archéologie et langage*, Flammarion, Paris, 1994.

[RHA 09] RHALEM N., KHATTABI A., ACHOUR S. *et al.*, "Facteurs prédictifs de gravité de l'intoxication aux pesticides: expérience du Centre Antipoison du Maroc", *Annales de Toxicologie Analytique*, vol. 21, no. 2, pp. 79–84, 2009.

[ROM 86] ROMER P.M., "Increasing returns and long-run growth", *The Journal of Political Economy*, vol. 94, pp. 1002–1037, 1986.

[ROS 11] ROSOW K., HOLZAPFEL A., KARLAWISH J.-H. *et al.*, "Countrywide strategic plans on Alzheimer's disease: developing the framework for the international battle against Alzheimer's Disease", *Alzheimer & Dementia*, vol. 7, pp. 615–621, 2011.

[ROU 55] ROUSSEAU J.-J., *Discours sur l'origine et les fondements de l'inégalité parmi les hommes* (cited from Gallimard, Paris, 1965), 1755.

[SAD 14] SADI N.E., "Biotechnologies de la santé: un business model en pleine mutation", *Harvard Business Review*, France, April 2014.

[SAD 15] SADI N.E., "Le financement des firmes de biotechnologie santé: un enjeu économique et financier central", in LECOINTRE G. (ed.), *Le Grand Livre de l'économie des PME*, vol. 3, Gualino, 2015.

[SAL 89] SALAIS R., "L'analyse économique des conventions de travail", *Revue économique*, vol. 40, no. 2, pp. 199–240, March 1989.

[SAP 98] SAPOLSKY R., "The physiology of dominance in stable versus unstable social hierarchies", in MASON W.A., MENDOZA S.P. (eds), *Primate Social Conflict*, State University of New York Press, Albany, 1998.

[SCH 00] SCHWEDER R.A., "The psychology of practice and the practice of the three psychologies", *Asian Journal of Social Psychology*, vol. 3, no. 3, pp. 207–222, 2000.

[SEB 16] SEBAI J., "Une analyse théorique de la coordination dans le domaine des soins: application aux systèmes de soins coordonnés", *Santé Publique*, vol. 28, no. 2, pp. 223–234, 2016.

[SEM 04] SEMLALI I., SOULAYMANI R., Rapport d'activité de toxico vigilance du Centre Anti-Poison du Maroc (CAPM) (1992–2003), Centre Anti-Poison et de Pharmacovigilance du Maroc, Rabat, 2004.

[SHI 15] SHI L., MAKINEN M., LEE D.C. *et al.*, "Integrated care delivery and health care seeking by chronically-ill patients – a case–control study of rural Henan province, China", *International Journal for Equity in Health*, vol. 14, no. 1, p. 98, 2015.

[SHO 92] SHOWERS C., "The motivational and emotional consequences of considering positive or negative possibilities for an upcoming event", *Journal of Personality and Social Psychology*, vol. 63, pp. 474–484, 1992.

[SIG 14] SIGURGEIRSDÓTTIR S., WAAGFJÖRÐ J., MARESSO A., "Iceland: health system review", *Health Systems in Transition*, vol. 16, no. 6, pp. 1–182, 2014.

[SIM 55] SIMON H.A., "A behavioural model of rational choice", *Quarterly Journal of Economics*, vol. 69, pp. 99–118, 1955.

[SIM 79] SIMON H.A., "Rational decision making in business organizations", *American Economic Review*, vol. 69, pp. 493–513, September 1979.

[SIM 91] SIMON H.A., "Organizations and markets", *Journal of Economic Perspectives*, vol. 5, no. 2, pp. 25–44, 1991.

[SOL 56] SOLOW R.M., "A contribution to the theory of economic growth", *The Quarterly Journal of Economics*, vol. 70, pp. 65–94, 1956.

[SRI 92] SRIAMPORN S., VATANASAPT V., PISANI P. *et al.*, "Environmental risk factors for nasopharyngeal carcinoma: a case–control study in northeastern Thailand", *Cancer Epidemiology Biomarkers & Prevention*, vol. 1, no. 5, pp. 345–348, 1992.

[STR 15] STRÖHLE A., SCHMIDT D.K., SCHULTZ F. *et al.*, "Drug and exercise treatment of Alzheimer disease and mild cognitive impairment: a systematic review and meta-analysis of effects on cognition in randomized controlled trials", *The American Journal of Geratric Psychiatry*, vol. 23, no. 12, pp. 1234–1249, 2015.

[TAY 88] TAYLOR S.E., BROWN J.D., "Illusion and well-being: a social psychological perspective on mental health", *Psychological Bulletin*, vol. 103, pp. 193–210, 1988.

[TAY 92] TAYLOR S.E., KEMENY M.E., ASPINVALL L.G. *et al.*, "Optimism, coping, psychological distress, and high-risk sexual behaviour among men at risk for AIDS", *Journal of Personality and Social Psychology*, vol. 53, pp. 460–473, 1992.

[TRO 12] TRONTO J., *Le risque ou le care?*, PUF, Paris, 2012.

[TSA 14] TSAI T.-C., "When Hippocrates and Sun Simiao met in Taiwan in a highly efficient health care system", *Medical Education*, vol. 48, no. 1, pp. 14–48, 2014.

[VAN 92] VAN DER VELDE F.W., VAN DER PLIGT J., HOOYKAAS C., "Risk perception and behaviour: pessimism, realism, and optimism about AIDS-related health behaviour", *Psychology and Health*, vol. 6, pp. 23–28, 1992.

[VAU 80] VAUGHN R., "How advertising works: a planning model", *Journal of Advertising Research*, vol. 20, no. 5, pp. 27–33, 1980.

[WEI 80] WEINSTEIN N.D., "Unrealistic optimism about future life events", *Journal of Personality and Social Psychology*, vol. 39, pp. 806–820, 1980.

[WEI 95] WEINSTEIN N.D., KLEIN W.M., "Resistance of personal risk perceptions to debiasing interventions", *Health Psychology*, vol. 14, pp. 132–140, 1995.

[WHI 16] WHITING S. *et al.*, "Moving towards universal health coverage through the development of integrated service delivery packages for primary health care in the Solomon Islands", *International Journal of Integrated Care*, vol. 16, no. 1, p. 3, 2016.

[WHO 78] WHO, "Declaration of Alma-Ata", International Conference on Primary Health Care, available at: www.who.int/publications/almaata_declaration_en.pdf, Alma-Ata, USSR, 6–12 September 1978.

[WHO 15] WHO, "Framework on integrated, people-centred health services", International Conference on Primary Health Care, Document OMS EB 138/37, available at: http://apps.who.int/gb/ebwha/pdf_files/EB138/B138_37-en.pdf, 18 December 2015.

[WIL 02] WILKINSON R., *L'inégalité nuit gravement à la santé*, Cassini, Paris, 2002.

[WIL 10] WILKINSON R., *L'égalité c'est la santé*, Demopolis, Paris, 2010.

[ZEN 15] ZENG L., WANG N., WANG Q. *et al.*, "Oral Chinese herbal medicine for kidney nourishment in Alzheimer disease", *Complementaries Therapies in Medicine*, vol. 23, no. 2, pp. 283–297, 2015.

[ZOU 15] ZOU Y., ZHANG X., HUO Y. *et al.*, "GP versus other physicians in the quality of primary care: a cross-sectional study in Guangdong Province, China", *BMC Family Practice*, vol. 16, p. 134, 2015.

Co-author and collaborator bibliographic references

[CAL 16a] CALLENS S., GNASSOU J., "Entre médiation et régulation: quelle résilience pour les Objectifs du Développement Durable?", in FERREOL G. (ed.), *Médiations et régulations*, EME, Louvain-la-Neuve, 2016.

[CAL 16b] CALLENS S., "Amputations: un cycle de l'éthique médicale", *Ethique et économique*, vol. 13, no. 1, pp. 75–93, 2016.

[CAL 16c] CALLENS S., *Catastrophe et résilience*, EUE, Sarrebruck, 2016.

[CAL 15] CALLENS S., "Ulrich Beck (1944–2015) et la société mondiale du risque", *Développement durable et territoires*, vol. 6, no. 1, 2015.

[CAL 14] CALLENS S., "Stratégies d'adaptation dans l'espace saharo-sahélien", in FERREOL G. (éd.) *Risque et vulnérabilité*, EME, Brussels, 2014.

[CAL 12] CALLENS S., SHANG L., "Haïti, ou les deux limites des ONG", *Préludes. Les cahiers de l'Association Tiers Monde*, vol. 27, pp. 175–184, 2012.

[CAL 08] CALLENS S., BARBE P., "L'origine des inégalités. Religion et innovation à l'âge du cuivre", *Innovations*, vol. 1, no. 27, pp. 11–25, 2008.

[CAL 96] CALLENS S., "La mesure du risque: une histoire récente", *Revue Française des Affaires Sociales*, vol. 2, pp. 73–83, 1996.

[DEL 13] DELAUCHE M.-C., BLACKWELL N., LE PERFF H. *et al.*, "A prospective study of the outcome of patients with limb trauma following the Haitian Earthquake in 2010 at One- and Two- Year (The SuTra^2 Study)", *PLOS Currents Disasters*, 5 July 2013.

Ethical codes

[NAT 15] NATIONAL ASSOCIATION OF GERIATRIC CARE MANAGERS, Code of Ethics, 2015.

[ESP 11] ESPACE NATIONAL DE REFLEXION ETHIQUE SUR LA MALADIE D'ALZHEIMER, Charte Alzheimer, 2011.

Index

Printed in the United States
By Bookmasters